TITLE 234

RULES OF CRIMINAL PROCEDURE

Editorial Note

Under the Commonwealth Documents Law the text of documents published in this title acquires no special status by reason of such publication. For the official text of judicial documents reference should be made to the Prothonotary of the Supreme Court or to the Administrative Office of Pennsylvania Courts, as appropriate. See 201 Pa. Code Rule 103.

Source

The provisions of this Title 234 reorganized and renumbered March 1, 2000, effective April 1, 2001, 30 Pa.B. 1477, unless otherwise noted.

Preface

The following rules were rescinded during the renumbering and reorganization of the Rules of Criminal Procedure. The rule numbers and their Comment, Official Notes and Committee Explanatory Reports are printed here for history purposes. See 30 Pa.B. 1477, 1486 (March 18, 2000).

Rule 27. [Rescinded].

Official Note: Formerly Rule 143, adopted January 31, 1970, effective May 1, 1970; renumbered Rule 27 September 18, 1973, effective January 1, 1974; amended February 15, 1974, effective immediately; Comment revised March 22, 1989, effective July 1, 1989; amended June 19, 1996, effective July 1, 1996; rescinded March 1, 2000, effective April 1, 2001, and replaced by Rule 112.

Committee Explanatory Reports:

Final Report explaining the June 19, 1996 amendments published with the Court's Order at 26 Pa.B. 3128 (July 6, 1996).

Final Report explaining the March 1, 2000 reorganization and renumbering of the rules published with the Court's Order at 30 Pa.B. 1478 (March 18, 2000).

1-1

Rule 39. [Rescinded].

Official Note: Rule 39 adopted October 1, 1997, effective October 1, 1998; rescinded March 1, 2000, effective April 1, 2001, and replaced by Rule 1101.

Committee Explanatory Reports:

Final Report explaining the provisions of new Rule 39 published with the Court's Order at 27 Pa.B. 5405 (October 18, 1997).

Final Report explaining the March 1, 2000 reorganization and renumbering of the rules published with the Court's Order at 30 Pa.B. 1478 (March 18, 2000).

Rule 86. [Rescinded].

Official Rule: Rule 86 adopted July 12, 1985, effective January 1, 1986; revised September 23, 1985, effective January 1, 1986; January 1, 1986 effective dates extended to July 1, 1986; amended February 2, 1989, effective March 1, 1989; amended March 22, 1993, effective January 1, 1994; amended October 28, 1994, effective as to cases instituted on or after January 1, 1995; amended February 27, 1995, effective July 1, 1995; amended October 1, 1997, effective October 1, 1998; amended May 14, 1999, effective July 1, 1999; rescinded March 1, 2000 and paragraphs (A), (D), (E), (F), and (I) replaced by Rule 460, paragraphs (B) and (C) replaced by Rule 461, and paragraph (G) replaced by Rule 462, effective April 1, 2001.

Committee Explanatory Reports:

Final Report explaining the March 22, 1993 amendments published with the Court's Order at 23 Pa.B. 1699 (April 10, 1993).

Final Report explaining the October 28, 1994 amendments published with the Court's Order at 24 Pa.B. 5843 (November 26, 1994).

Final Report explaining the February 27, 1995 amendments published with the Court's Order at 25 Pa.B. 935 (March 18, 1995).

Final Report explaining the October 1, 1997 amendments published with the Court's Order at 27 Pa.B. 5408 (October 18, 1997).

Final Report explaining the May 14, 1999 amendments to paragraph (G) concerning the police officer's presence published with the Court's Order at 29 Pa.B. 2776 (May 29, 1999).

Final Report explaining the March 1, 2000 reorganization and renumbering of the rules published with the Court's Order at 30 Pa.B. 1478 (March 18, 2000).

Rule 90. [Rescinded].

Official Note: Rule 90 adopted July 12, 1985, effective January 1, 1986; effective date extended to July 1, 1986; rescinded March 1, 2000 and replaced by Rule 109, effective April 1, 2001.

Committee Explanatory Reports:

Final Report explaining the March 1, 2000 reorganization and renumbering of the rules published with the Court's Order at 30 Pa.B. 1478 (March 18, 2000).

Rule 150. [Rescinded].

Official Note: Previous paragraph (a) (Informal Defects) formerly Rule 114 and previous paragraph (b) (Substantive Defects) formerly Rule 115, both adopted June 30, 1964, effective January 1, 1965; suspended January 31, 1970, effective May 1, 1970; revised January 31, 1970, effective May 1, 1970; combined renumbered Rule 150, and amended September 18, 1973, effective January 1, 1974; amended April 8, 1982, effective July 1, 1983; Comment revised July 12, 1985, effective January 1, 1986; effective date extended to July 1, 1986; rescinded March 1, 2000 and replaced by Rule 109, effective April 1, 2001.

Committee Explanatory Reports:

Final Report explaining the March 1, 2000 reorganization and renumbering of the rules published with the Court's Order at 30 Pa.B. 1478 (March 18, 2000).

Rule 159. [Rescinded].

Official Note: Rule 159 adopted September 18, 1973, effective January 1, 1974; amended January 28, 1983, effective July 1, 1983; amended February 1, 1989, effective July 1, 1989; amended April 10, 1989, effective July 1, 1989; amended January 31, 1991, effective July 1, 1991; rescinded March 1, 2000 and replaced by Rule 1101, effective April 1, 2001.

Committee Explanatory Report:

Report explaining the January 31, 1991 amendments published at 20 Pa.B. 4788 (September 15, 1990); Supplemental Report published at 21 Pa.B. 621 (February 16, 1991).

Final Report explaining the March 1, 2000 reorganization and renumbering of the rules published with the Court's Order at 30 Pa.B. 1478 (March 18, 2000).

Rule 328. [Rescinded].

Official Note: Rule 328 adopted January 25, 1971, effective February 1, 1971; amended June 29, 1977 and November 22, 1977, effective as to cases in which the indictment or information is filed on or after January 1, 1978; Comment revised March 22, 1989, effective July 1, 1989; rescinded and replaced by new Rule 112 March 1, 2000, effective April 1, 2001.

Committee Explanatory Reports:

Final Report explaining the March 1, 2000 reorganization and renumbering of the rules published with the Court's Order at 30 Pa.B. 1478 (March 18, 2000).

Rule 340. [Rescinded].

Official Note: Rule 340 combined former Rules 321 and 322, which were the previous suspension rules. Adopted June 29, 1977, effective September 1, 1977; amended April 24, 1981, effective June 1, 1981; amended January 28, 1983, effective July 1, 1983; rescinded and replaced by Rule 1101 March 1, 2000, effective April 1, 2001.

Committee Explanatory Reports:

Final Report explaining the March 1, 2000 reorganization and renumbering of the rules published with the Court's Order at 30 Pa.B. 1478 (March 18, 2000).

1-3

Rule 1415. [Rescinded].

Official Note: Rule 1415 adopted July 23, 1973, effective 90 days hence; paragraph (g) added March 21, 1975, effective March 31, 1975; amended August 14, 1995, effective January 1, 1996; rescinded and replaced by Rule 1101 March 1, 2000, effective April 1, 2001.

Committee Explanatory Reports:

Final Report explaining the August 14, 1995 amendments published with the Court's Order at 25 Pa.B. 3472 (August 26, 1995).

Final Report explaining the March 1, 2000 reorganization and renumbering of the rules published with the Court's Order at 30 Pa.B. 1478 (March 18, 2000).

Rule 2020. [Rescinded].

Official Note: Rule adopted September 3, 1993, effective January 1, 1994; rescinded March 1, 2000, effective April 1, 2001, and replaced by Rule 1101.

Committee Explanatory Reports:

Report explaining the provisions of the new rule published at 21 Pa.B. 3681 (August 17, 1991).

Final report explaining the March 1, 2000 reorganization and renumbering of the rules published with the Court's Order at 30 Pa.B. 1478 (March 18, 2000).

CHAPTER 1. SCOPE OF RULES, CONSTRUCTION AND DEFINITIONS, LOCAL RULES

PART A. Business of the Courts

PART B. Counsel

PART C. Venue, Location, and Recording of Proceedings Before Issuing Authority

PART D. Procedures Implementing 42 Pa.C.S. §§ 4137, 4138, and 4139: Criminal Contempt Powers of District Justices, Judges of the Pittsburgh Magistrates Court, and Judges of the Traffic Court of Philadelphia

PART E. Miscellaneous Warrants

Rule 100. Scope of Rules.

(A) These rules shall govern criminal proceedings in all courts including courts not of record. Unless otherwise specifically provided, these rules shall not apply to juvenile or domestic relations proceedings.

(B) Each of the courts exercising criminal jurisdiction may adopt local rules of procedure in accordance with Rule 105.

Comment

Under the 1974 amendment, the Pennsylvania Rules of Criminal Procedure, formerly inapplicable to summary cases in Philadelphia, now apply to such cases as specified in Chapter 10.

These rules apply to proceedings involving juveniles only to the extent that the Juvenile Act does not vest jurisdiction in the Juvenile Court, and as provided in the Rules of Juvenile Court Procedure. *See, e.g.*, Juvenile Act, 42 Pa.C.S. §§ 6302—6303, 6355; Vehicle Code, 75 Pa.C.S. § 6303, and Rules of Juvenile Court Procedure 105 (Search Warrants), 395 (Procedure to Initiate Criminal Information), and 396 (Bail). These rules also apply to cases in which an individual under the age of 18 allegedly commits a crime but the charges are not filed until the individual is 21 and therefore outside the Juvenile Act's definition of child. *See* 42 Pa.C.S. § 6302. *See also Commonwealth v. Monaco*, 869 A.2d 1026 (Pa. Super. 2005).

(372093) No. 477 Aug. 14

Official Note: Prior rule suspended effective May 1, 1970. Present Rule 1 adopted January 31, 1970, effective May 1, 1970; amended April 26, 1972, effective immediately; amended June 28, 1974, effective July 1, 1974; amended January 28, 1983, effective July 1, 1983; Comment revised July 12, 1985, effective January 1, 1986; effective date extended to July 1, 1986; renumbered Rule 100 and amended March 1, 2000, effective April 1, 2001; Comment revised April 1, 2005, effective October 1, 2005; Comment revised January 18, 2013, effective May 1, 2013.

Committee Explanatory Reports:

Final Report explaining the March 1, 2000 reorganization and renumbering of the rules published with the Court's Order at 30 Pa.B. 1478 (March 18, 2000).

Final Report explaining the April 1, 2005 Comment revision concerning Rules of Juvenile Court Procedure published with the Court's Order at 35 Pa.B. 2213 (April 16, 2005).

Final Report explaining the January 18, 2013 Comment revision concerning application of Criminal Rules to cases involving individuals under the age of 18 at time of offense and over 21 at time charges filed published with the Court's Order at 43 Pa.B. 653 (February 2, 2013).

Source

The provisions of this Rule 100 amended April 1, 2005, effective October 1, 2005, 35 Pa.B. 2210; amended January 18, 2013, effective May 1, 2013, 43 Pa.B. 652. Immediately preceding text appears at serial pages (360823) to (360824).

Rule 101. Purpose and Construction.

(A) These rules are intended to provide for the just determination of every criminal proceeding.

(B) These rules shall be construed to secure simplicity in procedure, fairness in administration, and the elimination of unjustifiable expense and delay.

(C) To the extent practicable, these rules shall be construed in consonance with the rules of statutory construction.

Comment

These rules were adopted under the Act of July 11, 1957, P. L. 819, 17 P. S. 2084 (Supp.), which was repealed by JARA, 42 P. S. § 20002(a), and replaced by 42 Pa.C.S. § 1722(a)(1).

Official Note: Rule 2 adopted June 30, 1964, effective January 1, 1965; renumbered Rule 101 and amended March 1, 2000, effective April 1, 2001.

Committee Explanatory Reports:

Final Report explaining the March 1, 2000 reorganization and renumbering of the rules published with the Court's Order at 30 Pa.B. 1478 (March 18, 2000).

Rule 102. Citing the Criminal Procedural Rules.

All criminal procedural rules adopted by the Supreme Court under the authority of Article V 10(c) of the Constitution of Pennsylvania, adopted April 23, 1968, shall be known as the Pennsylvania Rules of Criminal Procedure and shall be cited as "Pa.R.Crim.P. ."

Official Note: Rule 4 adopted March 20, 1972, effective immediately; amended September 18, 1973, effective January 1, 1974; renumbered Rule 102 March 1, 2000, effective April 1, 2001.

1-6

Committee Explanatory Reports:

Final Report explaining the March 1, 2000 reorganization and renumbering of the rules published with the Court's Order at 30 Pa.B. 1478 (March 18, 2000).

PART A. Business of the Courts

Rule 103. Definitions.

The following words and phrases, when used in any Rule of Criminal Procedure, shall have the following meanings:

ADVANCED COMMUNICATION TECHNOLOGY is any communication equipment that is used as a link between parties in physically separate locations, and includes, but is not limited to: systems providing for two-way simultaneous communication of image and sound; closed-circuit television; telephone and facsimile equipment; and electronic mail.

ADVANCED COMMUNICATION TECHNOLOGY SITE is any approved location within Pennsylvania designated by the president judge, or the president judge's designee, with advanced communication technology equipment that is available for parties in a criminal matter to communicate with others in physically separate locations as provided in these rules.

AFFIANT is any responsible person capable of taking an oath who signs, swears to, affirms, or, when permitted by these rules, verifies a complaint and appreciates the nature and quality of that person's act.

ARRAIGNMENT is the pretrial proceeding in the court of common pleas conducted pursuant to Rule 571.

BAIL is the security or other guarantee required and given for the release of a person, conditioned upon a written undertaking, in the form of a bail bond, that the person will appear when required and comply with all conditions set forth in the bail bond.

BAIL AUTHORITY is the magisterial district judge, magistrate, Philadelphia arraignment court magistrate, or the judge with jurisdiction over the case who is authorized by law to set, modify, revoke, or deny bail.

CAPITAL CASE or **CRIME** is one in or for which the death penalty may be imposed.

CARRIER SERVICE includes, but is not limited to, delivery by companies such as Federal Express or United Parcel Service, or a local courier service, and courthouse interoffice mail. The courthouse interoffice mail is a method of delivery used in some judicial districts for transmittal of documents between offices in the courthouse, and between the courthouse and other county facilities, including the county jail facility.

CLERK OF COURTS is that official, without regard to that person's title, in each judicial district who, pursuant to 42 **Pa.C.S.** §§ 2756 and 2757, has the responsibility and function to maintain the official criminal case file and list of docket entries, and to perform such other duties as required by rule or law.

COLLATERAL is cash or a cash equivalent deposited in summary cases.

1-7

COPY is an exact duplicate of an original document, including any required signatures, produced through mechanical or electronic means, and includes, but is not limited to: carbon copies; copies reproduced by using a photocopy machine, by transmission using facsimile equipment, or by scanning into and printing out of a computer.

COURT is a court of record.

COURT ADMINISTRATOR is that official in each judicial district who has the responsibility for case management and such other responsibilities as provided by the court.

COURT CASE is a case in which one or more of the offenses charged is a misdemeanor, felony, or murder of the first, second, or third degree.

CRIMINAL PROCEEDINGS include all actions for the enforcement of the Penal Laws.

INDICTMENT is the instrument holding the defendant for court after a grand jury votes to indict and authorizing the attorney for the Commonwealth to prepare an information.

INFORMATION is a formal written statement charging the commission of an offense signed and presented to the court by the attorney for the Commonwealth after a defendant is held for court, is indicted by the grand jury, or waives the preliminary hearing or a grand jury proceeding.

ISSUING AUTHORITY is any public official having the power and authority of a magistrate, a Philadelphia arraignment court magistrate, or a magisterial district judge.

LAW ENFORCEMENT OFFICER is any person who is by law given the power to enforce the law when acting within the scope of that person's employment.

MOTION includes any challenge, petition, application, or other form of request for an order or relief.

ORDINANCE is a legislative enactment of a political subdivision.

PENAL LAWS include all statutes and embodiments of the common law which establish, create, or define crimes or offenses, including any ordinances which may provide for imprisonment upon conviction or upon failure to pay a fine or penalty.

POLICE OFFICER is any person who is by law given the power to arrest when acting within the scope of the person's employment.

POLITICAL SUBDIVISION shall mean county, city, township, borough, or incorporated town or village having legislative authority.

PRELIMINARY ARRAIGNMENT is the proceeding following an arrest conducted before an issuing authority pursuant to Rule 540 or Rule 1003(D).

SEALED VERDICT is a verdict unanimously agreed upon by the jury, completed, dated, and signed by the foreman of the jury, and closed to open view.

SECURITY shall include cash, certified check, money order, personal check, or guaranteed arrest bond or bail bond certificate.

1-8

SIGNATURE, when used in reference to documents generated by the minor judiciary or court of common pleas, includes a handwritten signature, a copy of a handwritten signature, a computer generated signature, or a signature created, transmitted, received, or stored by electronic means, by the signer or by someone with the signer's authorization, unless otherwise provided in these rules.

SUMMARY CASE is a case in which the only offense or offenses charged are summary offenses.

VOIR DIRE is the examination and interrogation of prospective jurors.

Comment

The definitions of arraignment and preliminary arraignment were added in 2004 to clarify the distinction between the two proceedings. Although both are administrative proceedings at which the defendant is advised of the charges and the right to counsel, the preliminary arraignment occurs shortly after an arrest before a member of the minor judiciary, while an arraignment occurs in the court of common pleas after a case is held for court and an information is filed.

The definition of indictment was amended in 2012 consistent with the adoption of the new indicting grand jury rules in Chapter 5 Part E. Under the new rules, the indictment is the functional equivalent of an issuing authority's order holding the defendant for court and that forms the basis for the information that is prepared by the attorney for the Commonwealth. Formerly, an indictment was defined as a bill of indictment that has been approved by a grand jury and properly returned to court, or which has been endorsed with a waiver as provided in former Rule 215.

The definition of information was added to the rules as part of the implementation of the 1973 amendment to PA. CONST. art. I, § 10, permitting the substitution of informations for indictments. The term "information" as used here should not be confused with prior use of the term in Pennsylvania practice as an instrument which served the function now fulfilled by the complaint.

The definitions of bail authority and issuing authority were amended in 2005 to reflect the provisions of Act 207 of 2004 that changed the phrase "district justice" to "magisterial district judge," effective January 29, 2005. *See also* the Court's January 6, 2005 Order providing that any reference to "district justice" in a court rule shall be deemed a reference to a "magisterial district judge."

The definitions of "bail authority" and "issuing authority" were amended in 2009 to reflect the provisions of Act 98 of 2008 that changed the phrase "bail commissioner" to "arraignment court magistrate," effective December 8, 2008. *See also* the Court's January 21, 2009 Order providing that any reference to "bail commissioner" in a court rule shall be deemed a reference to an "arraignment court magistrate."

Neither the definition of law enforcement officer nor the definition of police officer gives the power of arrest to any person who is not otherwise given that power by law.

See Rule 1036 for the definition of hearing officers of the Philadelphia Municipal Court Traffic Division as "issuing authorities" for limited purposes specified in the rule.

The definition of signature was added in 2004 to make it clear when a rule requires a document generated by the minor judiciary or court of common pleas to include a signature or to be signed, that the signature may be in any of the forms provided in the definition. In addition, documents that institute proceedings or require the inclusion of an oath ordinarily are not documents generated by the minor courts or courts of common pleas and therefore any signature required on the document would not be included in this definition of signature; however, in the event such a document is generated by the minor courts or the courts of common pleas, the form of "signature" on this document is limited to handwritten, and the other forms of signature provided in the definition are not permitted.

1-9

Included in Chapter 5 Part C of the rules are additional definitions of words and phrases that apply specifically to bail in criminal cases. *See, e.g.*, Rule 524, which defines the types of release on bail.

Official Note: Previous Rules 3 and 212 adopted June 30, 1964, effective January 1, 1965, suspended January 31, 1970, effective May 1, 1970; present Rule 3 adopted January 31, 1970, effective May 1, 1970; amended June 8, 1973, effective July 1, 1973; amended February 15, 1974, effective immediately; amended June 30, 1977, effective September 1, 1977; amended January 4, 1979, effective January 9, 1979; amended July 12, 1985, effective January 1, 1986; January 1, 1986 effective date extended to July 1, 1986; amended August 12, 1993, effective September 1, 1993; amended February 27, 1995, effective July 1, 1995; amended September 13, 1995, effective January 1, 1996. The January 1, 1996 effective date extended to April 1, 1996; the April 1, 1996 effective date extended to July 1, 1996; renumbered Rule 103 and Comment revised March 1, 2000, effective April 1, 2001; amended May 10, 2002, effective September 1, 2002; amended March 3, 2004, effective July 1, 2004; amended April 30, 2004, effective July 1, 2004; amended August 24, 2004, effective August 1, 2005; amended February 4, 2005, effective immediately; amended May 6, 2009, effective immediately; amended June 21, 2012, effective in 180 days; Comment revised May 7, 2014, effective immediately.

Committee Explanatory Reports:

Report explaining the August 12, 1993 amendments published at 22 Pa.B. 3826 (July 25, 1992).

Final Report explaining the February 27, 1995 amendments published with the Court's Order at 25 Pa.B. 935 (March 18, 1995).

Final Report explaining the September 13, 1995 amendments published with Court's Order at 25 Pa.B. 4116 (September 30, 1995).

Final Report explaining the March 1, 2000 reorganization and renumbering of the rules published with the Court's Order at 30 Pa.B. 1478 (March 18, 2000).

Final Report explaining the May 10, 2002 amendments concerning advanced communication technology published with the Court's Order at 32 Pa.B. 2591 (May 25, 2002).

Final Report explaining the March 3, 2004 amendments defining carrier service, clerk of courts, court administrator, and motion published with the Court's Order at 34 Pa.B. 1561 (March 20, 2004).

Final Report explaining the April 30, 2004 amendments defining "signature" published with the Court's Order at 34 Pa.B. 2542 (May 15, 2004).

Final Report explaining the August 24, 2004 amendments adding definitions of arraignment and preliminary arraignment published with the Court's Order at 34 Pa.B. 5025 (September 11, 2004).

Final Report explaining the February 4, 2005 amendments modifying the definitions of bail authority and issuing authority published with the Court's Order at 35 Pa.B. 1333 (February 19, 2005).

Final Report explaining the May 6, 2009 amendments modifying the definitions of bail authority and issuing authority published with the Court's Order at 39 Pa.B. 2567 (May 23, 2009).

Final Report explaining the June 21, 2012 amendments modifying the definitions of "indictment" and "information" published with the Court's Order at 42 Pa.B. 4153 (July 7, 2012).

Final Report explaining the May 7, 2014 revision of the Comment cross-referencing the Rule 1036 limited definition of Philadelphia Municipal Court Traffic Division hearing officers as "issuing authorities" published with the Court's Order at 44 Pa.B. 3056 (May 24, 2014).

Source

The provisions of this Rule 103 amended May 10, 2002, effective September 1, 2002, 32 Pa.B. 2582; amended March 3, 2004, effective July 1, 2004, 34 Pa.B. 1547; amended April 30, 2004, effective July 1, 2004, 34 Pa.B. 2541; amended August 24, 2004, effective August 1, 2005, 34 Pa.B. 5016; amended February 4, 2005, effective immediately, 35 Pa.B. 1331; amended May 22, 2009, effective immediately, 39 Pa.B. 2567; amended June 21, 2012, effective in 180 days, 42 Pa.B. 4140; amended May 7, 2014, effective immediately, 44 Pa.B. 3056. Immediately preceding text appears at serial pages (361811) to (361814).

Rule 104. Design of Forms.

The Court Administrator of Pennsylvania, in consultation with the Criminal Procedural Rules Committee, shall design and publish forms necessary to implement these Rules.

> **Official Note:** Formerly Rule 144, adopted January 31, 1970, effective May 1, 1970; amended and renumbered Rule 5 September 18, 1973, effective January 1, 1974; amended July 12, 1985, effective January 1, 1986; effective date extended to July 1, 1986; renumbered Rule 104 March 1, 2000, effective April 1, 2001.

Committee Explanatory Reports:

Final Report explaining the March 1, 2000 reorganization and renumbering of the rules published with the Court's Order at 30 Pa.B. 1477 (March 18, 2000).

Rule 105. Local Rules.

Procedures for the promulgation and amendment of local criminal procedural rules are set forth in Pennsylvania Rule of Judicial Administration 103(d).

Comment

In 2016, the Supreme Court of Pennsylvania unified and consolidated the requirements and procedures for the promulgation and amendment of all local procedural rules, including local criminal procedural rules, into Pennsylvania Rule of Judicial Administration 103(d). All local rules previously promulgated in accordance with the requirements of Pa.R.Crim.P. 105 prior to this amendment remain effective upon compilation and publication pursuant to Pa.R.J.A. No. 103(d)(7).

> **Official Note:** Rule 6 adopted January 28, 1983, effective July 1, 1983; amended May 19, 1987, effective July 1, 1987; renumbered Rule 105 and amended March 1, 2000, effective April 1, 2001; amended October 24, 2000, effective January 1, 2001; Comment revised June 8, 2001, effective immediately; amended October 15, 2004, effective January 1, 2005; amended September 9, 2005, effective February 1, 2006; amended January 25, 2008, effective February 1, 2009; amended January 30, 2009, effective February 1, 2009; amended May 7, 2014, effective immediately; rescinded June 28, 2016, effective August 1, 2016. New Rule 105 adopted June 28, 2016, effective August 1, 2016.

Committee Explanatory Reports:

Final Report explaining the March 1, 2000 reorganization and renumbering of the rules published with the Court's Order at 30 Pa.B. 1478 (March 18, 2000).

Final Report explaining the October 24, 2000 amendments published with the Court's Order at 30 Pa.B. 5742 (November 11, 2000).

Final Report explaining the June 8, 2001 Comment revision citing to the AOPC's webpage published with the Court's Order at 31 Pa.B. 3310 (June 23, 2001).

Final Report explaining the October 15, 2004 amendment to paragraph (A), and to paragraph (C)(3) concerning the Legislative Reference Bureau publication requirements, published with the Court's Order at 34 Pa.B. 5893 (October 30, 2004).

Final Report explaining the September 9, 2005 amendments to paragraph (A) published with the Court's Order at 35 Pa.B. 5242 (September 24, 2005).

Final Report explaining the January 25, 2008 changes to Rule 105 concerning submission of local rules for review prior to adoption published with the Court's Order at 38 Pa.B. 746 (February 9, 2008).

Final Report explaining the January 30, 2009 changes to Rule 105 concerning publication of local rules on the UJS Portal published with the Court's Order at 39 Pa.B. 829 (February 14, 2009).

Final Report explaining the May 7, 2014 amendments concerning the transfer of the Philadelphia Traffic Court functions to the Philadelphia Municipal Court published with the Court's Order at 44 Pa.B. 3056 (May 24, 2014).

Final Report explaining the June 28, 2016 rescission of Rule 105, adoption of new Rule 105, and the consolidation of the local rulemaking approval and adoption procedures in Pa.R.J.A.103(d) published with the Court's Order at 46 Pa.B. 3807 (July 16, 2016).

Source

The provisions of this Rule 105 amended October 24, 2000, effective January 1, 2001, 30 Pa.B. 5841; amended June 8, 2001, effective immediately, 31 Pa.B. 3310; amended October 18, 2004, effective January 1, 2005, 34 Pa.B. 5892; amended September 9, 2005, effective February 1, 2006, 35 Pa.B. 5239; amended February 8, 2008, effective February 1, 2009, 38 Pa.B. 745; amended January 30, 2009, effective as to all local criminal rules adopted or amended on or after February 1, 2009; amended May 7, 2014, effective immediately, 44 Pa.B. 3056; rescinded and replaced June 28, 2016, effective August 1, 2016, 46 Pa.B. 3806. Immediately preceding text appears at serial pages (372099) to (372102).

Rule 106. Continuances in Summary and Court Cases.

(A)   The court or issuing authority may, in the interests of justice, grant a continuance, on its own motion, or on the motion of either party.

(B)   When the matter is before an issuing authority, the issuing authority shall record on the transcript the identity of the moving party and the reasons for granting or denying the continuance.

(C)   When the matter is in the court of common pleas, the judge shall on the record identify the moving party and state of record the reasons for granting or denying the continuance. The judge also shall indicate on the record to which party the period of delay caused by the continuance shall be attributed and whether the time will be included in or excluded from the computation of the time within which trial must commence in accordance with Rule 600.

(D)   A motion for continuance on behalf of the defendant shall be made not later than 48 hours before the time set for the proceeding. A later motion shall be entertained only when the opportunity therefor did not previously exist, or the defendant was not aware of the grounds for the motion, or the interests of justice require it.

(E)   When a continuance is granted, the notice of the new date, time, and location of the proceeding shall be served on the parties as provided in these rules.

Comment

For the procedures for filing and service of court orders and notices in general, see Rule 114. For the procedures for service of the continuance of a preliminary hearing, see Rule 542(G)(2).

Official Note: Rule 301 adopted June 30, 1964, effective January 1, 1965; amended June 8, 1973, effective July 1, 1973; amended June 29, 1977 and November 22, 1977, effective as to cases in which the indictment or information is filed on or after January 1, 1978; renumbered Rule 106 and amended March 1, 2000, effective April 1, 2001; amended October 1, 2012, effective July 1, 2013.

Committee Explanatory Reports:

Final Report explaining the March 1, 2000 reorganization and renumbering of the rules published with the Court's Order at 30 Pa.B. 1478 (March 18, 2000).

Final Report explaining the July 1, 2012 amendments to paragraphs (B) and (C) concerning Rule 600 and paragraph (E) concerning service published with the Court's Order at 42 Pa.B. 6629 (October 20, 2012).

Source

The provisions of this Rule 106 amended October 1, 2012, effective July 1, 2013, 42 Pa.B. 6622. Immediately preceding text appears at serial pages (343841) and (335923).

Rule 107. Contents of Subpoena.

A subpoena in a criminal case shall order the witness named to appear before the court at the date, time, and place specified, and to bring any items identified or described. The subpoena shall also state on whose behalf the witness is being ordered to testify and the identity, address, and phone number of the attorney, if any, who applied for the subpoena.

Comment

The form of subpoena was deleted in 1985 because it is no longer necessary to control the specific form of subpoena by rule.

It is intended that the subpoena shall be used not only for trial but also for any other stage of the proceedings when a subpoena is issuable, including preliminary hearings, hearings in connection with pretrial and post-trial motions, etc.

When the subpoena is for the production of documents, records, or things, these should be specified.

Official Note: Previous Rule 9016 adopted January 28, 1983, effective July 1, 1983; rescinded November 9, 1984, effective January 2, 1985. Present Rule 9016 adopted November 9, 1984, effective January 2, 1985; renumbered Rule 107 and amended March 1, 2000, effective April 1, 2001.

Committee Explanatory Reports:

Final Report explaining the March 1, 2000 reorganization and renumbering of the rules published with the Court's Order at 30 Pa.B. 1478 (March 18, 2000).

Rule 108. Habeas Corpus Venue.

(A) A petition for writ of habeas corpus challenging the legality of the petitioner's detention or confinement in a criminal matter shall be filed with the clerk of courts of the judicial district in which the order directing the petitioner's detention or confinement was entered.

(B) A petition for writ of habeas corpus challenging the conditions of the petitioner's confinement in a criminal matter shall be filed with the clerk of courts of the judicial district in which the petitioner is confined.

Comment

This rule implements Section 6502(b) of the Judicial Code as it applies to the venue for petitions for writs of habeas corpus in criminal matters, 42 Pa.C.S. § 6502(b). The rule is not intended to affect existing law concerning the availability and scope of habeas corpus relief. The rule also is not intended to apply to proceedings authorized by law for post-conviction remedies. See Section 6503 of the Judicial Code, 42 Pa.C.S. § 6503.

Separate petitions are required under this rule when the petitioner is confined in one judicial district due to an order entered in another judicial district and seeks to challenge both the legality and the conditions of confinement. A petition misfiled in the wrong judicial district under this rule may be transferred to the proper judicial district pursuant to Section 5103 of the Judicial Code, 42 Pa.C.S. § 5103(a).

Official Note: Rule 1701 adopted December 11, 1980, effective April 1, 1981; renumbered Rule 108 and amended March 1, 2000, effective April 1, 2001.

Committee Explanatory Reports:

Final Report explaining the March 1, 2000 reorganization and renumbering of the rules published with the Court's Order at 30 Pa.B. 1478 (March 18, 2000).

Rule 109. Deffects in Form, Content, or Procedure.

A defendant shall not be discharged nor shall a case be dismissed because of a defect in the form or content of a complaint, citation, summons, or warrant, or a defect in the procedures of these rules, unless the defendant raises the defect before the conclusion of the trial in a summary case or before the conclusion of the preliminary hearing in a court case, and the defect is prejudicial to the rights of the defendant.

Comment

This rule combines and replaces former Rules 90 and 150.

This rule clarifies when a defendant should be discharged or a case dismissed because of a defect; it eliminates disputes as to what is an informal defect or a substantive defect. As a condition of relief regardless of whether the defect is in form, content, or procedure, the court or issuing authority must determine that there is actual prejudice to the rights of the defendant.

A complaint, citation, summons, or warrant may be amended at any time so as to remedy any defect in form or content that is not prejudicial to the rights of the defendant. Nothing in this rule shall prevent the filing of a new complaint or citation and the reissuance of process. Any new complaint or citation must be filed within the time permitted by the applicable statute of limitations.

Ordinarily, if a defendant does not raise a defect at the summary trial or before the conclusion of the preliminary hearing, the defendant cannot thereafter raise the defect as grounds for dismissal or discharge at a later stage in the proceedings. See *Commonwealth v. Krall*, 452 Pa. 215, 304 A.2d 488 (1973). In a summary case, however, the provisions of this rule do not preclude a defendant from raising a defect for the first time after the summary trial when the interests of justice require it, as for example, when the defendant was not represented by counsel during the proceedings before the district justice or when the defendant could not reasonably have discovered the defect until after the conclusion of the summary trial.

Any defect properly raised under this rule shall be specifically described on the docket by the issuing authority. See Pa.R.Crim.P. 135.

If the issuing authority determines that a defect is prejudicial, it is intended that the decision recorded on the docket pursuant to Rule 135(B)(13) shall be "discharge of the defendant" or "dismissal of the case," rather than "not guilty."

Official Note: Former Rule 90 adopted July 12, 1985, effective January 1, 1986; effective date extended to July 1, 1986; rescinded March 1, 2000, effective April 1, 2001, and replaced by Rule 109. Former Rule 150, formed from former Rule 114 (Informal Defects), and former Rule 115 (Substantive Defects), both adopted June 30, 1964, effective January 1, 1965; suspended effective May 1, 1970; both revised January 31, 1970, effective May 1, 1970; combined, renumbered Rule 150 and amended September 18, 1973, effective January 1, 1974; amended April 8, 1982, effective July 1, 1982, Comment revised July 12, 1985, effective January 1, 1986; effective date extended to July 1, 1986; rescinded March 1, 2000, effective April 1, 2001, and replaced by Rule 109. New Rule 109 adopted March 1, 2000, effective April 1, 2001; Comment revised July 10, 2008, effective February 1, 2009.

Committee Explanatory Reports:

Final Report explaining the March 1, 2000 reorganization and renumbering of the rules, and the provisions of Rule 109, published with the Court's Order at 30 Pa.B. 1477 (March 18, 2000).

Final Report explaining the July 10, 2008 revisions to the Comment related to the cross-reference to Rule 135, published with the Court's Order at 38 Pa.B. 3975 (July 26, 2008).

Source

The provisions of this Rule 109 amended July 10, 2008, effective February 1, 2009, 38 Pa.B. 3971. Immediately preceding text appears at serial pages (264118) and (289061).

Rule 110. Special Orders Governing Widely-Publicized or Sensational Cases.

In a widely-publicized or sensational case, the court, on motion of either party or on its own motion, may issue a special order governing such matters as extra-judicial statements by parties and witnesses likely to interfere with the rights of the accused to a fair trial by an impartial jury, the seating and conduct in the courtroom of spectators and news media representatives, the management and sequestration of jurors and witnesses, and any other matters that the court may deem appropriate for inclusion in such an order. In such cases, it may be appropriate for the court to consult with representatives of the news media concerning the issuance of such a special order.

Official Note: Rule 326 adopted January 25, 1971, effective February 1, 1971; amended June 29, 1977 and November 22, 1977, effective as to cases in which the indictment or information is filed on or after January 1, 1978; renumbered Rule 110 and amended March 1, 2000, effective April 1, 2001.

Committee Explanatory Reports:

Final Report explaining the March 1, 2000 reorganization and renumbering of the rules published with the Court's Order at 30 Pa.B. 1477 (March 18, 2000).

Rule 111. Public Discussion of Pending or Imminent Criminal Litigation by Court Personnel.

All court personnel including, among others, court clerks, bailiffs, tipstaffs, and court stenographers are prohibited from disclosing to any person, without authorization by the court, information relating to a pending criminal case that is not part of the public records of the court. This rule specifically prohibits the divulgence of information concerning arguments and hearings held in chambers or otherwise outside the presence of the public.

> **Official Note:** Rule 327 adopted January 25, 1971, effective February 1, 1971; amended June 29, 1977 and November 22, 1977, effective as to cases in which the indictment or information is filed on or after January 1, 1978; renumbered Rule 111 and amended March 1, 2000, effective April 1, 2001.

Committee Explanatory Reports:

> Final Report explaining the March 1, 2000 reorganization and renumbering of the rules published with the Court's Order at 30 Pa.B. 1477 (March 18, 2000).

Rule 112. Publicity, Broadcasting, and Recording of Proceedings.

(A) The court or issuing authority shall:

(1) prohibit the taking of photographs, video, or motion pictures of any judicial proceedings or in the hearing room or courtroom or its environs during the judicial proceedings; and

(2) prohibit the transmission of communications by telephone, radio, television, or advanced communication technology from the hearing room or the courtroom or its environs during the progress of or in connection with any judicial proceedings, whether or not the court is actually in session.

The environs of the hearing room or courtroom is defined as the area immediately surrounding the entrances and exits to the hearing room or courtroom.

(B) The court or issuing authority may permit the taking of photographs, or radio or television broadcasting, or broadcasting by advanced technology, of judicial proceedings, such as naturalization ceremonies or the swearing in of public officials, which may be conducted in the hearing room or courtroom.

(C) Except as provided in paragraph (D), the stenographic, mechanical, electronic recording, or the recording using any advanced communication technology, of any judicial proceedings by anyone other than the official court stenographer in a court case, for any purpose, is prohibited.

(D) In a judicial proceeding before an issuing authority, the issuing authority, the attorney for the Commonwealth, the affiant, or the defendant may cause a recording to be made of the judicial proceeding as an aid to the preparation of the written record for subsequent use in a case, but such recordings shall not be publicly played or disseminated in any manner unless in a court during a trial or hearing.

1-14

(E)   If it appears to the court or issuing authority that a violation of this rule has resulted in substantial prejudice to the defendant, the court or issuing authority, upon application by the attorney for the Commonwealth or the defendant, may:

(1)   quash the proceedings at the preliminary hearing and order another preliminary hearing to be held before the same issuing authority at a subsequent time without additional costs being taxed;

(2)   discharge the defendant on nominal bail if in custody, or continue the bail if at liberty, pending further proceedings;

(335927) No. 407 Oct. 08

1-14.2

(3)　order all costs of the issuing authority forfeited in the original proceedings; or

(4)　adopt any, all, or combination of these remedies as the nature of the case requires in the interests of justice.

Comment

This rule combines and replaces former Rules 27 and 328.

"Recording" as used in this rule is not intended to preclude the use of recording devices for the preservation of testimony as permitted by Rules 500 and 501.

The prohibitions under this rule are not intended to preclude the use of advanced communication technology for purposes of conducting court proceedings.

Official Note:　Former Rule 27, previously Rule 143, adopted January 31, 1970, effective May 1, 1970; renumbered Rule 27 September 18, 1973, effective January 1, 1974; amended February 15, 1974, effective immediately; Comment revised March 22, 1989, effective July 1, 1989; amended June 19, 1996, effective July 1, 1996; rescinded March 1, 2000, effective April 1, 2001, and replaced by Rule 112. Former Rule 328 adopted January 25, 1971, effective February 1, 1971; amended June 29, 1977 and November 22, 1977, effective as to cases in which the indictment or information is filed on or after January 1, 1978; Comment revised March 22, 1989, effective July 1, 1989; rescinded March 1, 2000, effective April 1, 2001, and replaced by Rule 112. New Rule 112 adopted March 1, 2000, effective April 1, 2001; amended May 10, 2002, effective September 1, 2002.

Committee Explanatory Reports:

FORMER RULE 27:

Final Report explaining the June 19, 1996 amendments to former Rule 27 published with the Court's Order at 26 Pa.B. 3128 (July 6, 1996).

NEW RULE 112:

Final Report explaining the March 1, 2000 reorganization and renumbering of the rules, and the provisions of Rule 112, published at 30 Pa.B. 1477 (March 18, 2000).

Final Report explaining the May 10, 2002 amendments published with the Court's Order at 32 Pa.B. 2591 (May 25, 2002).

Source

The provisions of this Rule 112 amended May 10, 2002, effective September 1, 2002, 32 Pa.B. 2582. Immediately preceding text appears at serial pages (264120) to (264121).

Rule 113. Notice of Court Proceeding(s) Requiring Defendant's Presence. [Reserved].

Official Note:　Former Rule 9024 adopted October 21, 1983, effective January 1, 1984; amended March 22, 1993, effective as to cases in which the determination of guilt occurs on or after January 1, 1994; renumbered Rule 9025 June 2, 1994, effective September 1, 1994. New Rule 9024 adopted June 2, 1994, effective September 1, 1994; renumbered Rule 113 and amended March 1, 2000, effective April 1, 2001; rescinded March 3, 2004, and replaced by Rule 114(C), effective July 1, 2004.

1-15

Committee Explanatory Reports:

Report explaining the provisions of new Rule 9024 published at 23 Pa.B. 5008 (October 23, 1993).

Final Report explaining the March 1, 2000 reorganization and renumbering of the rules published with the Court's Order at 30 Pa.B. 1477 (March 18, 2000).

Final Report explaining the March 3, 2004 rescission of the rule published with the Court's Order at 34 Pa.B. 1561 (March 20, 2004).

Source

The provisions of this Rule 113 reserved March 3, 2004, effective July 1, 2004, 34 Pa.B. 1547. Immediately preceeding text appears at serial pages (289063) to (289064).

Rule 113. Criminal Case File and Docket Entries.

(A) The clerk of courts shall maintain the criminal case file for the court of common pleas. The criminal case file shall contain all original records, papers, and orders filed in the case, and copies of all court notices. These records, papers, orders, and copies shall not be taken from the custody of the clerk of court without order of the court. Upon request, the clerk shall provide copies at reasonable cost.

(B) The clerk of courts shall maintain a list of docket entries: a chronological list, in electronic or written form, of documents and entries in the criminal case file and of all proceedings in the case.

(C) The docket entries shall include at a minimum the following information:

(1)   the defendant's name;

(2)   the names and addresses of all attorneys who have appeared or entered an appearance, the date of the entry of appearance, and the date of any withdrawal of appearance;

(3)   notations concerning all papers filed with the clerk, including all court notices, appearances, pleas, motions, orders, verdicts, findings and judgments, and sentencings, briefly showing the nature and title, if any, of each paper filed, writ issued, plea entered, and motion made, and the substance of each order or judgment of the court and of the returns showing execution of process;

(4)   notations concerning motions made orally or orders issued orally in the courtroom when directed by the court;

(5)   a notation of every judicial proceeding, continuance, and disposition;

(6)   a notation if the defendant was under the age of 18 at the time of the commission of the alleged offense and charged with one of the offenses excluded from the definition of "delinquent act" in paragraphs (2)(i), (2)(ii), and (2)(iii) of 42 Pa.C.S. § 6302;

(7)   the location of exhibits made part of the record during the proceedings; and

(8)   all other information required by Rules 114 and 576.

1-16

Copyright © 2014 Commonwealth of Pennsylvania

Comment

This rule sets forth the mandatory contents of the list of docket entries and the criminal case files. This is not intended to be an exhaustive list of what is required to be recorded in the docket entries. The judicial districts may require additional information be recorded in a case or in all cases.

The list of docket entries is a running record of all information related to any action in a criminal case in the court of common pleas of the clerk's county, such as dates of filings, of orders, and of court proceedings. The clerk of courts is required to make docket entries at the time the information is made known to the clerk, and the practice in some counties of creating the list of docket entries only if an appeal is taken is inconsistent with this rule.

Nothing in this rule is intended to preclude the use of automated or other electronic means for time stamping or making docket entries.

This rule applies to all proceedings in the court of common pleas at any stage of a criminal case.

The requirement in paragraph (C)(2) that all attorneys and their addresses be recorded makes certain there is a record of all attorneys who have appeared for any litigant in the case. The requirement also ensures that attorneys are served as required in Rules 114 and 576. See also Rule 576(B)(4) concerning certificates of service.

In those cases in which the attorney has authorized receiving service by facsimile transmission or electronic means, the docket entry required in paragraph (C)(2) must include the facsimile number or electronic address.

Paragraph (C)(4) recognizes that occasionally disposition of oral motions presented in open court should be reflected in the docket, such as motions and orders related to omnibus pretrial motions (Rule 578), motions for a mistrial (Rule 605), motions for changes in bail (Rule 529), and oral motions for extraordinary relief (Rule 704(B)).

Unexecuted search warrants are not public records, see Rule 212(B), and therefore are not to be included in the criminal case file nor are they to be docketed.

> **Official Note:** Former Rule 9024 adopted October 21, 1983, effective January 1, 1984; amended March 22, 1993, effective as to cases in which the determination of guilt occurs on or after January 1, 1994; renumbered Rule 9025 June 2, 1994, effective September 1, 1994. New Rule 9024 adopted June 2, 1994, effective September 1, 1994; renumbered Rule 113 and amended March 1, 2000, effective April 1, 2001; rescinded March 3, 2004 and replaced by Rule 114(C), effective July 1, 2004. New Rule 113 adopted March 3, 2004, effective July 1, 2004; amended July 31, 2012, effective November 1, 2012; Comment revised October 22, 2013; effective January 1, 2014.

Committee Explanatory Reports:

Final Report explaining the provisions of the new rule published with the Court's Order at 34 Pa.B. 1561 (March 20, 2004).

Final Report explaining the July 31, 2012 amendment adding new paragraph (6) concerning defendants under the age of 18 published with the Court's Order at 42 Pa.B. 5340 (August 18, 2012).

Final Report explaining the October 22, 2013 revisions to the Comment regarding the unexecuted search warrants published with the Court's Order at 43 Pa.B. 6652 (November 9, 2013).

Source

The provisions of this Rule 113 adopted March 3, 2004, effective July 1, 2004, 34 Pa.B. 1547; amended July 31, 2012, effective November 1, 2012, 42 Pa.B. 5333; amended October 22, 2013, effective January 1, 2014, 43 Pa.B. 6649 Immediately preceding text appears at serial pages (363556) and (363557).

Rule 114. Orders and Court Notices: Filing; Service; and Docket Entries.

(A) Filing

(1)   All orders and court notices promptly shall be transmitted to the clerk of courts' office for filing. Upon receipt in the clerk of courts' office, the order or court notice promptly shall be time stamped with the date of receipt.

1-17

(2) All orders and court notices promptly shall be placed in the criminal case file.

(B) Service

(1) A copy of any order or court notice promptly shall be served on each party's attorney, or the party if unrepresented.

(2) The clerk of courts shall serve the order or court notice, unless the president judge has promulgated a local rule designating service to be by the court or court administrator.

(3) Methods of Service

Except as otherwise provided in Chapter 5 concerning notice of the preliminary hearing, service shall be:

    (a) in writing by

      (i) personal delivery to the party's attorney or, if unrepresented, the party; or

      (ii) personal delivery to the party's attorney's employee at the attorney's office; or

      (iii) mailing a copy to the party's attorney or leaving a copy for the attorney at the attorney's office; or

      (iv) in those judicial districts that maintain in the courthouse assigned boxes for counsel to receive service, when counsel has agreed to receive service by this method, leaving a copy for the party's attorney in the box in the courthouse assigned to the attorney for service; or

      (v) sending a copy to an unrepresented party by certified, registered, or first class mail addressed to the party's place of residence, business, or confinement; or

      (vi) sending a copy by facsimile transmission or other electronic means if the party's attorney, or the party if unrepresented, has filed a written request for this method of service as provided in paragraph (B)(3)(c); or

      (vii) delivery to the party's attorney, or the party if unrepresented, by carrier service; or

    (b) orally in open court on the record.

    (c) A party's attorney, or the party if unrepresented, may request to receive service of court orders or notices pursuant to this rule by facsimile transmission or other electronic means by

      (i) filing a written request for this method of service in the case or including a facsimile number or an electronic address on a prior legal paper filed in the case; or

      (ii) filing a written request for this method of service to be performed in all cases, specifying a facsimile number or an electronic address to which these orders and notices may be sent.

The request for electronic service in all cases filed pursuant to paragraph (ii) may be rescinded at any time by the party's attorney, or the party if unrepresented, by filing a written notice that service of orders and notices shall be accomplished as otherwise provided in this rule.

(C) Docket Entries

(1) Docket entries promptly shall be made.

(2) The docket entries shall contain:

    (a) the date of receipt in the clerk's office of the order or court notice;

    (b) the date appearing on the order or court notice; and

    (c) the date of service of the order or court notice.

(380190) No. 499 Jun. 16

Copyright © 2016 Commonwealth of Pennsylvania

(D) Unified Practice

Any local rule that is inconsistent with the provisions of this rule is prohibited, including any local rule requiring a party to file or serve orders or court notices.

Comment

This rule was amended in 2004 to provide in one rule the procedures for the filing and service of all orders and court notices, and for making docket entries of the date of receipt, date appearing on the order or notice, and the date of service. This rule incorporates the provisions of former Rule 113 (Notice of Court Proceedings Requiring Defendant's Presence). But see Rules 511, 540(F)(2), and 542(D) for the procedures for service of notice of a preliminary hearing, which are different from the procedures in this rule.

Historically, some orders or court notices have been served by the court administrator or by the court. Paragraph (B)(2) permits the president judge to continue this practice by designating either the court or the court administrator to serve orders and court notices. When the president judge makes such a designation, the designation must be in the form of a local rule promulgated in compliance with Rule 105 (Local Rules).

Paragraph (C)(2) requires three dates to be entered in the list of docket entries with regard to the court's orders and notices: the date of receipt of the order or notice; the date appearing on the order or notice; and the date the order or notice is served. The date of receipt is the date of filing under these rules. Concerning appeal periods and entry of orders, see Rule 720 (Post-Sentence Procedures; Appeal) and Pa.R.A.P. 108 (Date of Entry of Orders).

Court notices, as used in this rule, are communications that ordinarily are issued by a judge or the court administrator concerning, for example, calendaring or scheduling, including proceedings requiring the defendant's presence.

Although paragraph (B)(3)(a)(iv) permits the use of assigned mailboxes for service under this rule, the Attorney General's office never may be served by this method.

Paragraph (B)(3)(c) provides two methods for consenting to the receipt of orders and notices electronically. The first method, added to this rule in 2004, permits electronic service on a case-by-case basis with an authorization for such service required to be filed in each case. A facsimile number or an electronic address set forth on letterhead is not sufficient to authorize service by facsimile transmission or other electronic means under paragraph (B)(3)(c)(i). The authorization for service by facsimile transmission or other electronic means under this rule is valid only for the duration of the case. A separate authorization must be filed in each case the party or attorney wants to receive documents by this method of service.

The second method was added in 2010 to provide the option of entering a "blanket consent" to electronic service in all cases. It is expected that this would be utilized by those offices that work frequently in the criminal justice system, such as a district attorney's office or public defender's office, or by a judicial district that has the capability, based upon the availability of local technological resources, to accept a general request from a party to receive court orders and notices electronically. For example, a judicial district may have a system for electronically scanning documents that are stored on the courthouse computer system. In such a situation, an office that is part of the system, such as the District Attorney's Office or the Public Defender's Office, could consent to the receipt of all court orders and notices generally. As with service under paragraph (B)(3)(c)(i), a facsimile number or an electronic address set forth on letterhead is not sufficient to authorize service by facsimile transmission or other electronic means under paragraph (B)(3)(c)(ii). This consent may be rescinded as provided in paragraph (B)(3)(c).

Nothing in this rule is intended to preclude the use of automated or other electronic means for the transmission of the orders or court notices between the judge, court administrator, and clerk of courts, or for time stamping or making docket entries.

Nothing in this rule is intended to preclude a judicial district from utilizing the United States Postal Service's return receipt electronic option, or any similar service that electronically provides a return receipt, when using certified mail, return receipt requested.

Under the post-sentence motion procedures, the clerk of courts must comply with this rule after entering an order denying a post-sentence motion by operation of law. See Rule 720(B)(3)(c).

(354885) No. 436 Mar. 11

This rule makes it clear that the procedures for filing and service, and making docket entries are mandatory and may not be modified by local rule.

Paragraph (D), titled "Unified Practice," emphasizes that local rules must not conflict with the statewide rules. Although this prohibition on local rules that are inconsistent with the statewide rules applies to all Criminal Rules through Rule 105 (Local Rules), the reference to the specific prohibitions is included because these types of local rules have been identified by practitioners as creating significant impediments to the statewide practice of law within the unified judicial system. See the first paragraph of the Rule 105 Comment. The term "local rule" includes every rule, regulation, directive, policy, custom, usage, form or order of general application. See Rule 105(A).

For the definition of "carrier service," see Rule 103.

See Rule 103 for the definitions of "clerk of courts" and "court administrator."

See Rule 113 (Criminal Case File and Docket Entries) for the requirements concerning the contents of the criminal case file and the minimum information to be included in the docket entries.

Official Note: Formerly Rule 9024, adopted October 21, 1983, effective January 1, 1984; amended March 22, 1993, effective as to cases in which the determination of guilt occurs on or after January 1, 1994; renumbered Rule 9025 and Comment revised June 2, 1994, effective September 1, 1994; renumbered Rule 114 and Comment revised March 1, 2000, effective April 1, 2001; amended March 3, 2004, effective July 1, 2004; amended August 24, 2004, effective August 1, 2005; amended July 20, 2006, effective September 1, 2006; Comment revised September 18, 2008, effective February 1, 2009; amended December 6, 2010, effective February 1, 2011.

Committee Explanatory Reports:

Final Report explaining the March 22, 1993 amendments published with the Court's Order at 23 Pa.B. 1699 (April 10, 1993).

Report explaining the June 2, 1994 rule changes published at 23 Pa.B. 5008 (October 23, 1993).

Final Report explaining the March 1, 2000 reorganization and renumbering of the rules published with the Court's Order at 30 Pa.B. 1478 (March 18, 2000).

Final Report explaining the March 3, 2004 rule changes concerning filing and service, making docket entries, and orders and court notices published with the Court's Order at 34 Pa.B. 1561 (March 20, 2004).

Final Report explaining the August 24, 2004 changes concerning notice of preliminary hearing published with the Court's Order at 34 Pa.B. 5025 (September 11, 2004).

Final Report explaining the July 20, 2006 deletion of "manner of service" from paragraph (C)(2)(c) published with the Court's Order at 36 Pa.B. 4173 (August 5, 2006).

Final Report explaining the September 18, 2008 revision of the Comment concerning the United States Postal Service's return receipt electronic option published with the Court's Order at 38 Pa.B. 5428 (October 4, 2008).

Final Report explaining the December 6, 2010 amendment concerning consent to electronic service published with the Court's Order at 40 Pa.B. 7336 (December 25, 2010).

Source

The provisions of this Rule 114 amended March 3, 2004, effective July 1, 2004, 34 Pa.B. 1547; amended August 24, 2004, effective August 1, 2005, 34 Pa.B. 5016; amended July 20, 2006, effective September 1, 2006, 36 Pa.B. 4172; amended September 18, 2008, effective February 1, 2009, 38 Pa.B. 5425; amended December 6, 2010, effective February 1, 2011, 40 Pa.B. 7336. Immediately preceeding text appears at serial pages (321813) to (321814) and (338937) to (338938).

Rule 115. Recording and Transcribing Court Proceedings.

(A) In court cases, after a defendant has been held for court, proceedings in open court shall be recorded.

(B)   Upon the motion of any party, upon its own motion, or as required by law, the court shall determine and designate those portions of the record, if any, that are to be transcribed.

(C)   At any time before an appeal is taken the court may correct or modify the record in the same manner as is provided by Rule 1926 of the Pennsylvania Rules of Appellate Procedure.

Comment

Some form of record or transcript is necessary to permit meaningful consideration of claims of error and an adequate effective appellate review. See, e.g., Pa.Rs.A.P. 1922, 1923, 1924; *Commonwealth v. Fields*, 387 A.2d 83 (Pa. 1978); *Commonwealth v. Shields*, 383 A.2d 844 (Pa. 1978). No substantive change in law is intended by this rule, rather it is intended to provide a mechanism to insure appropriate recording and transcribing of court proceedings. For repeal of statutory provisions on this subject, see Judiciary Act Repealer Act § 2(a); 42 P. S. § 20002(a) [897], [944].

The rule is intended also to apply to proceedings that occur after the action that is the functional equivalent of holding a defendant for court in those cases in which it is permissible to proceed without a preliminary hearing and, therefore, without specifically holding the defendant for court. See Pa.Rs.Crim.P. 541, 550(D), 561, 565, 1010. In addition, the rule is intended to apply to de novo proceedings in the common pleas courts on appeals in summary cases. For application of the rule to proceedings in the Philadelphia Municipal Court, see Pa.R.Crim.P. 1012(A).

The rule is not intended to preclude adoption of local rules of court providing that arraignment need not be recorded, see Pa.R.Crim.P. 571, nor it is intended to modify any Rules of Criminal Procedure that specifically prohibit the recording or transcribing of all or part of a proceeding. See Pa.R-.Crim.P. 313. In addition, the rule is not meant to preclude the use of recording devices for the preservation of testimony under Pa.Rs.Crim.P. 500 and 501.

Paragraph (B) of the rule is intended to authorize courts to require transcription of only such portions of the record, if any, as are needed to review claims of error.

Paragraph (C) provides a method for correcting and modifying transcripts before appeal by incorporating Pa.R.A.P. 1926, which otherwise applies only after an appeal has been taken. It is intended that the same standards and procedures apply both before and after appeal.

   Official Note: Rule 9030 adopted April 24, 1981, effective July 1, 1981; Comment revised March 22, 1989, effective July 1, 1989; renumbered Rule 115 and amended March 1, 2000, effective April 1, 2001.

Committee Explanatory Reports:

Final Report explaining the March 1, 2000 reorganization and renumbering of the rules published with the Court's Order at 30 Pa.B. 1477 (March 18, 2000).

Rule 116. General Supervisory Powers of President Judge.

The President Judge shall be responsible for ensuring that the judicial district is in compliance with the Pennsylvania Rules of Criminal Procedure, other rules, and statutes, applicable to the minor judiciary, courts, clerks of courts, and court administrators.

Comment

By this rule, the Supreme Court is imposing on the president judges the responsibility of supervising their respective judicial districts to ensure compliance with the statewide Rules of Criminal Procedure, other rules, and statutes.

See 42 Pa.C.S. §§ 2756 and 2757 concerning the duties of the clerks of courts.

1-18.3

Official Note: Adopted March 3, 2004, effective July 1, 2004.

Committee Explanatory Reports:

Final Report explaining new Rule 116 published with the Court's Order at 34 Pa.B. 1561 (March 20, 2004).

Source

The provisions of this Rule 116 adopted March 3, 2004, effective July 1, 2004, 34 Pa.B. 1547.

Rule 117. Coverage: Issuing Warrants; Preliminary Arraignments and Summary Trials; and Setting and Accepting Bail.

(A) The president judge of each judicial district shall ensure sufficient availability of issuing authorities to provide the services required by the Rules of Criminal Procedure as follows:

(1) continuous coverage for the issuance of search warrants pursuant to Rule 203 and arrest warrants pursuant to Rule 513;

(2) coverage using one or a combination of the systems of coverage set forth in paragraph (B) to:

(a) conduct summary trials or set collateral in summary cases following arrests with a warrant issued pursuant to Rule 430(A) as provided in Rule 431(B)(3) and following arrests without a warrant as provided in Rule 441(C);

(b) conduct preliminary arraignments without unnecessary delay whenever a warrant of arrest is executed within the judicial district pursuant to Rule 516;

(c) set bail without unnecessary delay whenever an out-of-county warrant of arrest is executed within the judicial district pursuant to Rule 517(A);

(d) accept complaints and conduct preliminary arraignments without unnecessary delay whenever a case is initiated by an arrest without warrant pursuant to Rule 519(A)(1); and

(3) coverage during normal business hours for all other business.

(B) The president judge, taking into consideration the rights of the defendant and the judicial district's resources and coverage needs, by local rule promulgated pursuant to Rule 105, shall establish one or a combination of the following systems of coverage to provide the services enumerated in paragraph (A)(2):

(1) a traditional on-call system providing continuous coverage;

(2) an "after-hours court" or a "night court" staffed by an on-duty issuing authority and staff;

(3) a regional on-call system; or

(4) a schedule of specified times for after-hours coverage when the "duty" issuing authority will be available to conduct business.

(C) The president judge of each judicial district, by local rule promulgated pursuant to Rule 105, shall ensure that coverage is provided pursuant to Rule

1-18.4

520(B) to admit defendants to bail on any day and at any time in any case pending within the judicial district.

Comment

By this rule, the Supreme Court is clarifying the responsibility of president judges in supervising their respective judicial districts to ensure compliance with the statewide Rules of Criminal Procedure to prevent the violation of the rights of defendants caused by the lack of availability of the issuing authority. See also Rule 116 (General Supervisory Powers of President Judge) and Rule 131 (Location of Proceedings Before Issuing Authority).

Paragraph (A), derived from former Rule 132(A) (Continuous Availability), clarifies that it is the president judge's responsibility to make sure that there are issuing authorities available within his or her judicial district (1) on a continuous basis to issue search and arrest warrants, paragraph (A)(1); (2) pursuant to one or a combination of the systems of coverage enumerated in paragraph (B) to conduct summary trials and preliminary arraignments, and perform related duties, paragraph (A)(2); and (3) during normal business hours to conduct all other business of the minor judiciary, paragraph (A)(3). It is expected that the president judge will continue the established procedures in the judicial district or establish new procedures to ensure sufficient availability of issuing authorities consistent with this paragraph.

By providing the alternate systems of coverage in paragraph (B), this rule recognizes the differences in the geography and judicial resources of the judicial districts.

An issuing authority is "available" pursuant to paragraph (A) when he or she is able to communicate in person or by using advanced communication technology ("ACT") with the person requesting services pursuant to this rule. See Rule 103 for the definition of ACT. Concerning the use of ACT, see Rule 118 (Use of Two-Way Simultaneous Audio-Visual Communication in Criminal Proceedings). See also Rules 203, 513, 518, and 540 providing for the use of ACT to request and obtain warrants and conduct preliminary arraignments.

Nothing in this rule limits an issuing authority from exercising sound judicial discretion, within the parameters established by the president judge pursuant to paragraph (B), in deciding how to respond to a request for services outside normal business hours. See, e.g., Rule 509, paragraphs (1) and (2), that authorize the use of summonses instead of warrants in certain court cases; and Rule 519(B) that requires the police officer to release a defendant arrested without a warrant in certain specified court cases.

In determining which system of coverage to elect, the president judge must consider the rights of the defendant, see, e.g. *Commonwealth v. Duncan*, 514 Pa. 395, 525 A.2d 1177 (1987), and the judicial district's resources and coverage needs, as well as the obligations of the police and attorney for the Commonwealth to ensure the defendant is brought before an issuing authority without unnecessary delay as required by law, see, e.g., Rules 431, 441, 516, 517, and 519. See also *Commonwealth v. Perez*, 577 Pa. 360, 845 A.2d 779 (2004).

When the police must detain a defendant pursuant to these rules, 61 P. S. § 798 provides that the defendant may be housed for a period not to exceed 48 hours in "the borough and township lockups and city or county prisons."

The proceedings enumerated in paragraph (A)(2) include (1) setting bail before verdict pursuant to Rule 520(A) and Rule 540, and either admitting the defendant to bail or committing the defendant to jail, and (2) determining probable cause whenever a defendant is arrested without a warrant pursuant to Rule 540(E).

Pursuant to paragraph (C), the president judge also is responsible for making sure there is an issuing authority or other designated official available within the judicial district on a continuous basis to accept bail pursuant to Rule 520(B). The president judge, by local rule, may continue established procedures or establish new procedures for the after-hours acceptance of deposits of bail by an issuing authority, a representative of the office of the clerk of courts, or such other individual designated by

1-18.5

the president judge. See Rule 535(A). Given the complexities of posting real estate to satisfy a monetary condition of release, posting of real estate may not be feasible outside normal business hours.

When the president judge designates another official to accept bail deposits, that official's authority is limited under this rule to accepting the bail deposit, and under Rule 525 to releasing the defendant upon execution of the bail bond. Pursuant to Rule 535(A), the official is authorized only to have the defendant execute the bail bond and to deliver the bail deposit and bail bond to the issuing authority or clerk of courts.

The local rule requirements in paragraphs (B) and (C):

(1) ensure there is adequate notice of (a) the system of coverage, thereby providing predictability in the issuing authority's duty schedule, and (b) the official authorized to accept bail; (2) promote the efficient administration of justice; and (3) provide a means for the Supreme Court to monitor the times and manner of coverage in each judicial district.

The local rules promulgated pursuant to this rule should include other relevant information, such as what are the normal business hours of operation or any special locations designated by the president judge to conduct business, that will assist the defendants, defense counsel, attorneys for the Commonwealth, police, and members of the public.

Concerning other requirements for continuous coverage by issuing authorities in Protection from Abuse Act cases, see 23 Pa.C.S. § 6110 and Pa.R.C.P.D.J. 1203.

Official Note: Former Rule 117 adopted September 20, 2002, effective January 1, 2003; renumbered Rule 118 June 30, 2005, effective August 1, 2006. New Rule 117 adopted June 30, 2005, effective August 1, 2006; Comment revised July 31, 2012, effective November 1, 2012.

Committee Explanatory Reports:

Final Report explaining the provisions of the new rule published with the Court's Order at 35 Pa.B. 3911 (July 16, 2005).

Final Report explaining the July 31, 2012 revision of the Comment changing the citation to Rule 540(C) to Rule 540(E) published with the Court's Order at 42 Pa.B. 5340 (August 18, 2012).

Source

The provisions of this Rule 117 adopted June 30, 2005, effective August 1, 2006, 35 Pa.B. 3901; amended July 31, 2012, effective November 1, 2012, 42 Pa.B. 5333. Immediately preceding text appears at serial pages (354888) to (354890).

Rule 118. Court Fees Prohibited For Two-Way Simultaneous Audio-Visual Communication.

When a criminal proceeding is conducted by using two-way simultaneous audio-visual communication, the court shall not impose a fee upon the defendant for its use.

Comment

This rule implements the March 13, 2002 Order of the Supreme Court of Pennsylvania (No. 241 Judicial Administration; Doc. No. 1) that states, "No fees shall be imposed against a defendant in a criminal proceeding for the utilization of advanced communication technology." See 32 Pa.B. 1642 (March 30, 2002). When a criminal proceeding is conducted using two-way simultaneous audio-visual communication, this rule precludes the imposition of fees upon a defendant for the use of the two-way simultaneous audio-visual communication. See, e.g., Rules 540 (Preliminary Arraignment) and 571 (Arraignment). Two-way simultaneous audio-visual communication is a type of advanced communication technology as defined in Rule 103 (Definitions).

A "fee" as used in this rule includes, but is not limited to, a cost, charge, surcharge, and service charge.

Official Note: New Rule 117 adopted September 20, 2002, effective January 1, 2003; renumbered Rule 118 June 30, 2005, effective August 1, 2006.

1-18.6

Committee Explanatory Reports:

Final Report explaining new Rule 117 published with the Court's Order at 32 Pa.B. 4815 (October 4, 2002).

Final Report explaining the June 30, 2005 renumbering of Rule 117 as Rule 118 published with the Court's Order at 35 Pa.B. 3911 (July 16, 2005).

Source

The provisions of this Rule 118 adopted September 20, 2002, effective January 1, 2003, 32 Pa.B. 4814; amended June 30, 2005, effective August 1, 2006, 35 Pa.B. 3901. Immediately preceding text appears at serial pages (303623) to (303624).

Rule 119. Use of Two-Way Simultaneous Audio-Visual Communication in Criminal Proceedings.

(A) The court or issuing authority may use two-way simultaneous audio-visual communication at any criminal proceeding except:

    (1) preliminary hearings;

    (2) proceedings pursuant to Rule 569(A)(2)(b);

    (3) proceedings pursuant to Rules 595 and 597;

    (4) trials;

    (5) sentencing hearings;

    (6) parole, probation, and intermediate punishment revocation hearings; and

    (7) any proceeding in which the defendant has a constitutional or statutory right to be physically present.

(B) The defendant may consent to any proceeding being conducted using two-way simultaneous audio-visual communication.

(C) When counsel for the defendant is present, the defendant must be permitted to communicate fully and confidentially with defense counsel immediately prior to and during the proceeding.

Comment

This rule was adopted in 2003 to make it clear that unless the case comes within one of the exceptions in paragraph (A), the court or issuing authority may use two-way simultaneous audio-visual communication in any criminal proceeding. Two-way simultaneous audio-visual communication is a type of advanced communication technology as defined in Rule 103.

Nothing in this rule is intended to limit any right of a defendant to waive his or her presence at a criminal proceeding in the same manner as the defendant may waive other rights. *See, e.g.*, Rule 602 Comment. Negotiated guilty pleas when the defendant has agreed to the sentence, probation revocation hearings, and hearings held pursuant to Rule 908(C) and the Post Conviction Relief Act, 42 Pa.C.S. §§ 9541 et seq., are examples of hearings in which the defendant's consent to proceed using two-way simultaneous audio-visual communication would be required. Hearings on post-sentence motions, bail hearings, bench warrant hearings, extradition hearings, and *Gagnon* I hearings are examples of proceedings that may be conducted using two-way simultaneous audio-visual communication without the defendant's consent. It is expected the court or issuing authority would conduct a colloquy for the defendant's consent when the defendant's constitutional right to be physically present is implicated.

Within the meaning of this rule, counsel is present when physically with the defendant or with the judicial officer conducting the criminal proceeding.

This rule does not apply to preliminary arraignments (Rule 540), arraignments (Rule 571), or to search warrant (Rule 203) and arrest warrant (Chapter 5 Part B(3)) procedures.

This rule is not intended to preclude the use of advanced communication technology for the preservation of testimony as permitted by Rules 500 and 501.

See Rule 542 for the procedures governing preliminary hearings.

See Chapter 6 for the procedures governing trials.

See Chapter 7 for the procedures governing sentencing hearings.

See Rule 708 for the procedures governing revocation of probation, intermediate punishment, and parole.

The paragraph (A)(5) reference to revocation hearings addresses *Gagnon* II-type probation (*Gagnon v. Scarpelli*, 411 U.S. 778 (1973)) and parole (*Morrissey v. Brewer*, 408 U.S. 471 (1972)) revocation hearings, and is not intended to prohibit the use of two-way simultaneous audio-visual communication in hearings to determine probable cause (*Gagnon I*).

Official Note: New Rule 118 adopted August 7, 2003, effective September 1, 2003; renumbered Rule 119 and Comment revised June 30, 2005, effective August 1, 2006; amended January 27, 2006, effective August 1, 2006; Comment revised May 4, 2009, effective August 1, 2009; amended July 31, 2012, effective November 1, 2012.

Committee Explanatory Reports:

Final Report explaining new Rule 118 published with the Court's Order at 33 Pa.B. 4287 (August 30, 2003).

Final Report explaining the June 30, 2005 renumbering of Rule 118 as Rule 119 and the revision of the second paragraph of the Comment published at 35 Pa.B. 3911 (July 16, 2005).

Final Report explaining the January 27, 2006 amendments adding Rule 569 proceedings as a proceeding for which ACT may not be used published with the Court's Order at 36 Pa.B. 700 (February 11, 2006).

Final Report explaining the May 4, 2009 revision to the Comment adding PCRA hearings as a proceeding to which the defendant may consent to be held using ACT published with the Court's Order at 39 Pa.B. 2434 (May 16, 2009).

Final Report explaining the July 31, 2012 amendment to paragraph (A) adding proceedings under Rule 595 and 597 as a proceedings for which ACT may not be used published with the Court's Order at 42 Pa.B. 5340 (August 18, 2012).

Source

The provisions of this Rule 119 adopted August 7, 2003, effective September 1, 2003, 33 Pa.B. 4287; amended June 30, 2005, effective August 1, 2006, 33 Pa.B. 3901; amended January 27, 2006, effective August 1, 2006, 36 Pa.B. 694; amended May 4, 2009, effective immediately, 39 Pa.B. 2434; amended July 31, 2012, effective November 1, 2012, 42 Pa.B. 5333. Immediately preceding text appears at serial pages (360825) to (360826).

PART B. Counsel

Rule 120. Attorneys—Appearances and Withdrawals.

(A) ENTRY OF APPEARANCE

(1) Counsel for defendant shall file an entry of appearance with the clerk of courts promptly after being retained, and serve a copy of the entry of appearance on the attorney for the Commonwealth.

(a) If a firm name is entered, the name of an individual lawyer shall be designated as being responsible for the conduct of the case.

(b) The entry of appearance shall include the attorney's address, phone number, and attorney ID number.

(2) When counsel is appointed pursuant to Rule 122 (Appointment of Counsel), the filing of the appointment order shall enter the appearance of appointed counsel.

(3) Counsel shall not be permitted to represent a defendant following a preliminary hearing unless an entry of appearance is filed with the clerk of courts.

1-18.8

(4)   An attorney who has been retained or appointed by the court shall continue such representation through direct appeal or until granted leave to withdraw by the court pursuant to paragraph (B).

(B) WITHDRAWAL OF APPEARANCE

(1)   Counsel for a defendant may not withdraw his or her appearance except by leave of court.

(2)   A motion to withdraw shall be:

(a)   filed with the clerk of courts, and a copy concurrently served on the attorney for the Commonwealth and the defendant; or

(b)   made orally on the record in open court in the presence of the defendant.

(3)   Upon granting leave to withdraw, the court shall determine whether new counsel is entering an appearance, new counsel is being appointed to represent the defendant, or the defendant is proceeding without counsel.

Comment

Representation as used in this rule is intended to cover court appearances or the filing of formal motions. Investigation, interviews, or other similar pretrial matters are not prohibited by this rule.

For admission *pro hac vice*, see Pa.B.A.R. 301.

An attorney may not represent a defendant in a capital case unless the attorney meets the educational and experiential requirements set forth in Rule 801 (Qualifications for Defense Counsel in Capital Cases).

Paragraph (A)(2) was added in 2005 to make it clear that the filing of an order appointing counsel to represent a defendant enters the appearance of appointed counsel. Appointed counsel does not have to file a separate entry of appearance. Rule 122 (Appointment of Counsel) requires that (1) the judge include in the appointment order the name, address, and phone number of appointed counsel, and (2) the order be served on the defendant, appointed counsel, the previous attorney of record, if any, and the attorney for the Commonwealth pursuant to Rule 114 (Orders and Court Notices: Filing; Service; and Docket Entries).

Under paragraph (B)(2), counsel must file a motion to withdraw in all cases, and counsel's obligation to represent the defendant, whether as retained or appointed counsel, remains until leave to withdraw is granted by the court. *See, e.g., Commonwealth v. Librizzi*, 810 A.2d 692 (Pa. Super. Ct. 2002). The court must make a determination of the status of a case before permitting counsel to withdraw. Although there are many factors considered by the court in determining whether there is good cause to permit the withdrawal of counsel, when granting leave, the court should determine whether new counsel will be stepping in or the defendant is proceeding without counsel, and that the change in attorneys will not delay the proceedings or prejudice the defendant, particularly concerning time limits. In addition, case law suggests other factors the court should consider, such as whether (1) the defendant has failed to meet his or her financial obligations to pay for the attorney's services and (2) there is a written contractual agreement between counsel and the defendant terminating representation at a specified stage in the proceedings such as sentencing. *See, e.g., Commonwealth v. Roman. Appeal of Zaiser*, 549 A.2d 1320 (Pa. Super. Ct. 1988).

If a post-sentence motion is filed, trial counsel would normally be expected to stay in the case until disposition of the motion under the post-sentence procedures adopted in 1993. *See* Rules 704 and 720. Traditionally, trial counsel stayed in a case through post-verdict motions and sentencing.

For the filing and service procedures, see Rules 575-576.

(370029) No. 472 Mar. 14

For waiver of counsel, see Rule 121.

For the procedures for appointment of counsel, see Rule 122.

See Rule 904(A) that requires an attorney who has been retained to represent a defendant during post-conviction collateral proceedings to file a written entry of appearance.

Official Note: Adopted June 30, 1964, effective January 1, 1965; formerly Rule 303, renumbered Rule 302 and amended June 29, 1977 and November 22, 1977, effective as to cases in which the indictment or information is filed on or after January 1, 1978; amended March 22, 1993, effective January 1, 1994; renumbered Rule 120 and amended March 1, 2000, effective April 1, 2001; Comment revised February 26, 2002, effective July 1, 2002; Comment revised June 4, 2004, effective November 1, 2004; amended April 28, 2005, effective August 1, 2005; amended December 10, 2013, effective February 10, 2014.

Committee Explanatory Reports:

Final Report explaining the March 22, 1993 amendments published with the Court's Order at 23 Pa.B. 1699 (April 10, 1993).

Final Report explaining the March 1, 2000 reorganization and renumbering of the rules published with the Court's Order at 30 Pa.B. 1478 (March 18, 2000).

Final Report explaining the February 26, 2002 Comment revision adding the cross-reference to Rule 904 published with the Court's Order at 32 Pa.B. 1393 (March 16, 2002).

Final Report explaining the April 28, 2005 amendments concerning the filing of an appointment order as entry of appearance for appointed counsel and withdrawal of counsel published with the Court's Order at 35 Pa.B. 2859 (May 14, 2005).

Final Report explaining the December 10, 2013 change to the Comment published with the Court's Order at 43 Pa.B. 7546 (December 28, 2013).

Source

The provisions of this Rule 120 amended February 26, 2002, effective July 1, 2002, 32 Pa.B. 1391; amended June 4, 2004, effective November 1, 2004, 34 Pa.B. 3105; amended April 28, 2005, effective August 1, 2005, 35 Pa.B. 2855; amended December 10, 2013, effective February 10, 2014, 43 Pa.B. 7545. Immediately preceding text appears at serial pages (363562), (360827) to (360828) and (356639).

Rule 121. Waiver of Counsel.

(A)   GENERALLY.

(1)   The defendant may waive the right to be represented by counsel.

(2)   To ensure that the defendant's waiver of the right to counsel is knowing, voluntary, and intelligent, the judge or issuing authority, at a minimum, shall elicit the following information from the defendant:

(a)   that the defendant understands that he or she has the right to be represented by counsel, and the right to have free counsel appointed if the defendant is indigent;

(b)   that the defendant understands the nature of the charges against the defendant and the elements of each of those charges;

(c)   that the defendant is aware of the permissible range of sentences and/or fines for the offenses charged;

    (d)   that the defendant understands that if he or she waives the right to counsel, the defendant will still be bound by all the normal rules of procedure and that counsel would be familiar with these rules;

    (e)   that the defendant understands that there are possible defenses to these charges that counsel might be aware of, and if these defenses are not raised at trial, they may be lost permanently; and

    (f)   that the defendant understands that, in addition to defenses, the defendant has many rights that, if not timely asserted, may be lost permanently; and that if errors occur and are not timely objected to, or otherwise timely raised by the defendant, these errors may be lost permanently.

    (3)   The judge or issuing authority may permit the attorney for the Commonwealth or defendant's attorney to conduct the examination of the defendant pursuant to paragraph (A)(2). The judge or issuing authority shall be present during this examination.

(B) **PROCEEDINGS BEFORE AN ISSUING AUTHORITY.** When the defendant seeks to waive the right to counsel in a summary case or for a preliminary hearing in a court case, the issuing authority shall ascertain from the defendant whether this is a knowing, voluntary, and intelligent waiver of counsel. In addition, the waiver shall be in writing,

    (1)   signed by the defendant, with a representation that the defendant was told of the right to be represented and to have an attorney appointed if the defendant cannot afford one, and that the defendant chooses to act as his or her own attorney at the hearing or trial; and

    (2)   signed by the issuing authority, with a certification that the defendant's waiver was made knowingly, voluntarily, and intelligently.

The waiver shall be made a part of the record.

(C) **PROCEEDINGS BEFORE A JUDGE.** When the defendant seeks to waive the right to counsel after the preliminary hearing, the judge shall ascertain from the defendant, on the record, whether this is a knowing, voluntary, and intelligent waiver of counsel.

(D) **STANDBY COUNSEL.** When the defendant's waiver of counsel is accepted, standby counsel may be appointed for the defendant. Standby counsel shall attend the proceedings and shall be available to the defendant for consultation and advice.

Comment

Paragraph (A) recognizes that the right to self-representation is guaranteed by the sixth amendment to the Federal Constitution when a valid waiver is made, *Faretta v. California*, 422 U.S. 806 (1975).

In *Indiana v. Edwards*, 128 S.Ct. 2379, 2388 (2008), the Supreme Court recognized, as an exception to the right to self-representation, that, when a defendant is not mentally competent to conduct his or her own defense, the U.S. Constitution permits the judge to require the defendant to be represented by counsel.

(370031) No. 472 Mar. 14

The right of a defendant to waive counsel is not automatic. Under Pennsylvania's case law, the defendant's request must be clear and unequivocal. *See, e.g., Commonwealth v. Davido*, 582 Pa. 52, 64-65, 868 A.2d 431, 438, *cert. denied*, 546 U.S 1020 (2005).

Concerning when "meaningful trial proceedings" commence for purposes of a request to waive counsel for a bench trial, *see Commonwealth v. El*, 602 Pa. 126, 977 A.2d 1158 (2009). In *El*, the Court held that "meaningful trial proceedings" commence "when a court has begun to hear motions which have been reserved for time of trial; when oral arguments have commenced; or when some other such substantive first step in the trial has begun." *Id*, at 139, 977 A.2d at 1165, citing *Commonwealth v. Dowling*, 598 Pa. 611, 959 A.2d 910 (2008) (trial commences, for purposes of the right to a trial by jury, when the trial judge determines that the parties are present and directs them to proceed to opening argument, or to the hearing of any motions that had been reserved for the time of trial, or to some other such first step in the trial).

Court decisions contain broad language in referring to the areas and matters to be encompassed in determining whether the defendant understands the full impact and consequences of his or her waiver of the right to counsel, but is nevertheless willing to waive that right. The appellate courts require, however, at a minimum, that the judge or issuing authority ask questions to elicit the information set forth in paragraph (A)(2).

Although it is advisable that the judge or issuing authority conduct the examination of the defendant, the rule does not prevent the attorney for the Commonwealth or an already-appointed or retained defense counsel from conducting all or part of the examination of the defendant as permitted by the judge or issuing authority. See *Commonwealth v. McDonough*, 571 Pa. 232, 812 A.2d 504 (2002).

On the issue of waiver of counsel in general, see, e.g., *Commonwealth v. Tyler*, 468 Pa. 193, 360 A.2d 617 (1976); *Commonwealth ex rel. Fairman v. Cavell*, 423 Pa. 138, 222 A.2d 722 (1966) (mere execution of a waiver of counsel form, without more, is insufficient to establish a valid waiver); *Commonwealth ex rel. McCray v. Rundle*, 415 Pa. 65, 202 A.2d 303 (1964); *Commonwealth ex rel. O'Lock v. Rundle*, 415 Pa. 515, 204 A.2d 439 (1964).

On the issue of forfeiting the right to representation, see *Commonwealth v. Lucarelli*, 601 Pa. 185, 971 A.2d 1173 (2009), in which the Court held that Rule 121 and its colloquy requirements do not apply to situations in which forfeiture is found. The Court explained "where a defendant's course of conduct demonstrates his or her intention not to seek representation by private counsel, despite having the opportunity and financial wherewithal to do so, a determination that the defendant be required to proceed *pro se* is mandated because that defendant has forfeited the right to counsel." *Id.* at 195, 971 A.2d at 1179.

In referring to summary cases, paragraph (B) refers only to those summary cases in which there exists a right to counsel. See Rule 122.

While the rule continues to require a written waiver of counsel incorporating the contents specified in paragraph (B), in proceedings before an issuing authority, the form of waiver was deleted in 1985 because it is no longer necessary to control the specific form of written waiver by rule.

Under paragraph (C) of this rule, the colloquy relating to the defendant's attempted waiver of counsel must appear on the record. This requirement is not applicable to such waivers in proceedings under paragraph (B), because these proceedings are not in courts of record. However, the absence of such requirement is not intended to be construed as affecting the scope or nature of the inquiry to be made in a particular case.

It is intended that when the defendant has waived his or her right to counsel before the issuing authority for purposes of the preliminary hearing, such waiver shall not normally act as a waiver of the right to counsel in subsequent critical stages of the proceedings. Therefore, under paragraph (C) it is intended that a further waiver is subsequently to be taken by a judge of the court of common pleas.

With respect to trials in court cases, when the defendant waives the right to counsel and elects to proceed pro se, it is generally advisable that standby counsel be appointed to attend the proceedings and be available to the defendant for consultation and advice. See *Commonwealth v. Africa*, 466 Pa. 603, 353 A.2d 855 (1976). This is particularly true in cases expected to be long or complicated, or in which there are multiple defendants. See ABA Standards, The Function of the Trial Judge § 6.7 (Approved Draft 1972). The ability of standby counsel to assume control of the defense will minimize delay and disruption of the proceedings in the event that the defendant's self-representation terminates, e.g., either because such termination becomes necessary as a result of the defendant's unruly behavior, or because the defendant seeks to withdraw the waiver and be represented by counsel. With respect to pretrial proceedings or summary case trials it is intended that standby counsel may be appointed at the discretion of the presiding judicial officer.

Official Note: Rule 318 adopted October 21, 1977, effective January 1, 1978; amended November 9, 1984, effective January 2, 1985; renumbered Rule 121 and amended March 1, 2000, effective April 1, 2001; amended December 19, 2007, effective February 1, 2008; Comment revised March 29, 2011, effective May 1, 2011.

Committee Explanatory Reports:

Final Report explaining the March 1, 2000 reorganization and renumbering of the rules published with the Court's Order at 30 Pa.B. 1478 (March 18, 2000).

Final Report explaining the December 19, 2007 changes to paragraph (A) concerning areas of inquiry for waiver colloquy published with the Court's Order at 38 Pa.B. 62 (January 5, 2008).

Final Report explaining the March 29, 2011 changes to the Comment adding citations to recent case law concerning right to counsel, time for withdrawal of waiver, and forfeiture of right to counsel published with the Court's Order at 41 Pa.B. 2000 (April 16, 2011).

Source

The provisions of this Rule 121 amended December 19, 2007, effective February 1, 2008, 38 Pa.B. 61; amended March 29, 2011, effective May 1, 2011, 41 Pa.B. 1999. Immediately preceding text appears at serial pages (332091) to (332092) and (348259).

Rule 122. Appointment of Counsel.

(A) Counsel shall be appointed:

(1)   in all summary cases, for all defendants who are without financial resources or who are otherwise unable to employ counsel when there is a likelihood that imprisonment will be imposed;

(2)   in all court cases, prior to the preliminary hearing to all defendants who are without financial resources or who are otherwise unable to employ counsel;

(3)   in all cases, by the court, on its own motion, when the interests of justice require it.

(B) When counsel is appointed,

(1)   the judge shall enter an order indicating the name, address, and phone number of the appointed counsel, and the order shall be served on the defendant, the appointed counsel, the previous attorney of record, if any, and the attorney for the Commonwealth pursuant to Rule 114 (Orders and Court Notices: Filing; Service; and Docket Entries); and

(2)   the appointment shall be effective until final judgment, including any proceedings upon direct appeal.

(C) A motion for change of counsel by a defendant for whom counsel has been appointed shall not be granted except for substantial reasons.

Comment

This rule is designed to implement the decisions of *Argersinger v. Hamlin*, 407 U. S. 25 (1972), and *Coleman v. Alabama*, 399 U. S. 1 (1970), that no defendant in a summary case be sentenced to imprisonment unless the defendant was represented at trial by counsel, and that every defendant in a court case has counsel starting no later than the preliminary hearing stage.

No defendant may be sentenced to imprisonment or probation if the right to counsel was not afforded at trial. See *Alabama v. Shelton*, 535 U. S.654 (2002) and *Scott v. Illinois*, 440 U. S. 367 (1979). See Rule 454 (Trial in Summary Cases) concerning the right to counsel at a summary trial.

Copyright © 2011 Commonwealth of Pennsylvania

Appointment of counsel can be waived, if such waiver is knowing, intelligent, and voluntary. See *Faretta v. California*, 422 U. S. 806 (1975). Concerning the appointment of standby counsel for the defendant who elects to proceed pro se, see Rule 121.

In both summary and court cases, the appointment of counsel to represent indigent defendants remains in effect until all appeals on direct review have been completed.

Ideally, counsel should be appointed to represent indigent defendants immediately after they are brought before the issuing authority in all summary cases in which a jail sentence is possible, and immediately after preliminary arraignment in all court cases. This rule strives to accommodate the requirements of the Supreme Court of the United States to the practical problems of implementation. Thus, in summary cases, paragraph (A)(1) requires a pretrial determination by the issuing authority as to whether a jail sentence would be likely in the event of a finding of guilt in order to determine whether trial counsel should be appointed to represent indigent defendants. It is expected that the issuing authorities in most instances will be guided by their experience with the particular offense with which defendants are charged. This is the procedure recommended by the ABA Standards Relating to Providing Defense Services § 4.1 (Approved Draft 1968) and cited in the United States Supreme Court's opinion in *Argersinger*, supra. If there is any doubt, the issuing authority can seek the advice of the attorney for the Commonwealth, if one is prosecuting the case, as to whether the Commonwealth intends to recommend a jail sentence in case of conviction.

In court cases, paragraph (A)(2) requires counsel to be appointed at least in time to represent the defendant at the preliminary hearing. Although difficulty may be experienced in some judicial districts in meeting the *Coleman* requirement, it is believed that this is somewhat offset by the prevention of many post-conviction proceedings that would otherwise be brought based on the denial of the right to counsel. However, there may be cases in which counsel has not been appointed prior to the preliminary hearing stage of the proceedings, e.g., counsel for the preliminary hearing has been waived, or a then-ineligible defendant subsequently becomes eligible for appointed counsel. In such cases it is expected that the defendant's right to appointed counsel will be effectuated at the earliest appropriate time.

An attorney may not be appointed to represent a defendant in a capital case unless the attorney meets the educational and experiential requirements set forth in Rule 801 (Qualifications for Defense Counsel in Capital Cases).

Paragraph (A)(3) retains in the issuing authority or judge the power to appoint counsel regardless of indigency or other factors when, in the issuing authority's or judge's opinion, the interests of justice require it.

Pursuant to paragraph (B)(2) counsel retains his or her appointment until final judgment, which includes all avenues of appeal through the Supreme Court of Pennsylvania. In making the decision whether to file a petition for allowance of appeal, counsel must (1) consult with his or her client, and (2) review the standards set forth in Pa.R.A.P. 1114 (Considerations Governing Allowance of Appeal) and the note following that rule. If the decision is made to file a petition, counsel must carry through with that decision. See Commonwealth v. Liebel, 573 Pa. 375, 825 A.2d 630 (2003). Concerning counsel's obligations as appointed counsel, see *Jones v. Barnes*, 463 U.S. 745 (1983). See also *Commonwealth v. Padden*, 783 A.2d 299 (Pa. Super.2001).

See *Commonwealth v. Alberta*, 601 Pa. 473, 974 A.2d 1158 (2009), in which the Court stated that "[a]ppointed counsel who has complied with *Anders [v. California*, 386 U.S. 738 (1967),] and is permitted to withdraw discharges the direct appeal obligations of counsel. Once counsel is granted leave to withdraw per Anders, a necessary consequence of that decision is that the right to appointed counsel is at an end."

For suspension of Acts of Assembly, see Rule 1101.

Official Note: Rule 318 adopted November 29, 1972, effective 10 days hence, replacing prior rule; amended September 18, 1973, effective immediately; renumbered Rule 316 and amended June 29, 1977, and October 21, 1977, effective January 1, 1978; renumbered Rule 122 and amended March 1, 2000, effective April 1, 2001; amended March 12, 2004, effective July 1, 2004; Comment revised March 26, 2004, effective July 1, 2004; Comment revised June 4, 2004, effective November 1, 2004; amended April 28, 2005, effective August 1, 2005; Comment revised February 26, 2010, effective April 1, 2010.

Committee Explanatory Reports:

Final Report explaining the March 1, 2000 reorganization and renumbering of the rules published with the Court's Order at 30 Pa.B. 1477 (March 18, 2000).

Final Report explaining the March 12, 2004 editorial amendment to paragraph (C)(3), and the Comment revision concerning duration of counsel's obligation, published with the Court's Order at 34 Pa.B. 1671 (March 27, 2004).

Final Report explaining the March 26, 2004 Comment revision concerning *Alabama v. Shelton* published with the Court's Order at 34 Pa.B. 1929 (April 10, 2004).

Final Report explaining the April 28, 2005 changes concerning the contents of the appointment order published with the Court's Order at 35 Pa.B. 2855 (May 14, 2005).

Final Report explaining the February 26, 2010 revision of the Comment adding a citation to Commonwealth v. Alberta published at 40 Pa.B. 1396 (March 13, 2010).

Source

The provisions of this Rule 122 amended March 12, 2004, effective July 1, 2004, 34 Pa.B. 1671; amended March 26, 2004, effective July 1, 2004, 34 Pa.B. 1929; amended June 4, 2004, effective November 1, 2004, 34 Pa.B. 3105; amended April 28, 2005, effective August 1, 2005, 35 Pa.B. 2855; amended February 26, 2010, effective April 1, 2010, 40 Pa.B. 1396. Immediately preceeding text appears at serial pages (346779) to (346780) and (332095).

Rule 123. Application for the Assignment of Counsel.

A defendant who requests assignment of counsel in a court case shall file a signed and verified application for assignment of counsel, which shall set forth the facts showing that the defendant is without financial resources or is otherwise unable to employ counsel.

Comment

While this rule continues to require a written application for the assignment of counsel, the form of the application was deleted in 1985 because it is no longer necessary to control the specific form of written application by rule.

Official Note: Rule 318A adopted June 30, 1964, effective January 1, 1965; renumbered Rule 317 June 29, 1977 and November 22, 1977, effective as to cases in which the indictment or information is filed on or after January 1, 1978; rescinded November 9, 1984, effective January 2, 1985. Present Rule 317 adopted November 9, 1984, effective January 2, 1985; renumbered Rule 123 and title and Comment revised March 1, 2000, effective April 1, 2001.

Committee Explanatory Reports:

Final Report explaining the March 1, 2000 reorganization and renumbering of the rules published with the Court's Order at 30 Pa.B. 1477 (March 18, 2000).

Rule 124. In Forma Pauperis. [Reserved].

**PART C. Venue, Location, and Recording of Proceedings
before Issuing Authority**

Rule 130. Venue; Transfer of Proceedings.

(A) VENUE

All criminal proceedings in summary and court cases shall be brought before the issuing authority for the magisterial district which in the offense is alleged to have occurred or before an issuing authority on temporary assignment to serve such magisterial district, subject, however, to the following exceptions:

(1) A criminal proceeding may be brought before any issuing authority of any magisterial district within the judicial district whenever the particular place within the judicial district which the offense is alleged to have occurred in unknown.

(2) When changes arising from the same criminal episode occur in more than one magisterial district within the same judicial district, the criminal proceeding on all the charges should be brought before one issuing authority in any one of the magisterial districts in which the charges arising from the same criminal episode occurred.

(3) When charges arising from the criminal episode occur in more than one judicial district, the criminal proceeding on all the charges may be brought before one issuing authority in a magisterial district within any of the judicial districts in which the charges arising from the same criminal episode occurred.

(4) Whenever an arrest is made without a warrant for any summary offense arising under the Vehicle Code, which allegedly occurred on a highway of the Pennsylvania Turnpike System or any controlled or limited access highway, or any right-of-way of such System or highway, or any other highway or highways of the Commonwealth, the defendant shall be taken and the proceeding shall be brought either where the offense allegedly occurred, or before the issuing authority for any other magisterial district within the same judicial dis-

(356645) No. 440 Jul. 11

1-22.4

trict which, in the judgment of the arresting officer, is most convenient to the place of arrest without regard to the boundary line of any magisterial district or judicial district.

(5)   When any offense is alleged to have occurred within 100 yards of the boundary between two or more magisterial districts of a judicial district, the proceeding may be brought in either or any of the magisterial districts without regard of the boundary lines of any county.

(6)   When the president judge designates a magisterial district or a location in that district in which certain classes of offenses, which occurred in other specified magisterial districts, may be heard.

(B)   TRANSFER OF PROCEEDINGS IN COURT CASES

(1)   Prior to the completion of the preliminary hearing:

(a)   When charges arising from a single criminal episode, which occurred in more than one judicial district,

(i)   are filed in more than one judicial district, upon the filing with the issuing authority of a written agreement by the attorneys for the Commonwealth, the proceedings shall be transferred to the magisterial district in the judicial district selected by the attorneys for the Commonwealth; or

(ii)   are filed in one judicial district, upon the filing of a written agreement by the attorneys for the Commonwealth, the proceedings shall be transferred to the magisterial district in the judicial district selected by the attorneys for the Commonwealth.

(b)   When charges arising from a single criminal episode, which occurred in more than one magisterial district,

(i)   are filed in more than one magisterial district, the proceedings may be transferred to the magisterial district selected by the attorney for the Commonwealth; or

(ii)   are filed in one magisterial district, the proceedings may be transferred to another magisterial district selected by the attorney for the Commonwealth.

(2)   The issuing authority shall promptly transmit to the issuing authority of the magisterial district to which the proceedings are being transferred a certified copy of all docket entries, together with all the original papers filed in the proceeding, a copy of the bail bond and any deposits in satisfaction of a monetary condition of bail, and a bill of the costs which have accrued but have not been collected prior to the transfer.

Comment

When charges arising from a single criminal episode occur in more than one judicial district, the magisterial district in which the proceeding on all the charges is brought, i.e., the one with venue, may be any one of the magisterial districts in which the charges occurred. See *Commonwealth v. Geyer*, 687 A.2d 815 (Pa. 1996) (the compulsory joinder rule and 18 Pa.C.S. § 110 apply when two or more summary offenses arise from a single criminal episode).

1-23

Similarly, when charges arising from a single criminal episode occur in more than one magisterial district within one judicial district, the magisterial district in which the proceeding on all the charges is brought, i.e., the one with venue, may be any one of the magisterial districts in which the charges occurred.

The decision of in which magisterial district in paragraph (A)(2) or in which judicial district in paragraph (A)(3) the proceedings are to be brought is to made initially by the law enforcement officers or attorneys for the Commonwealth. In making the decision, the law enforcement officers or attorneys for the Commonwealth must consider in which magisterial district under paragraph (A)(2) or in which judicial district under paragraph (A)(3) it would be in the interests of justice to have the case proceed, based upon the convenience of the defendant and the witnesses, and the prompt administration of justice.

Venue is not altered when an issuing authority conducts a proceeding from an advanced communication technology site outside the issuing authority's magisterial district or judicial district.

See Rule 134 (Objections to Venue) for the procedures to challenge a transfer of proceedings under this rule.

See Rule 551 for the procedures to withdraw the prosecution.

See Chapter 5 Part C concerning bail.

Official Note: Formerly Rule 154, adopted January 16, 1970, effective immediately; section (a)(3) adopted July 1, 1970, effective immediately; renumbered Rule 21 September 18, 1973, effective January 1, 1974; amended July 1, 1980, effective August 1, 1980; amended January 28, 1983, effective July 1, 1983; renumbered Rule 130 and amended March 1, 2000, effective April 1, 2001; amended April 20, 2000, effective July 1, 2000; amended September 19, 2000, effective January 1, 2001; amended May 10, 2002, effective September 1, 2002; amended May 21, 2004, effective July 1, 2004.

Committee Explanatory Reports:

Final Report explaining the March 1, 2000 reorganization and renumbering of the rules published with the Court's Order at 30 Pa.B. 1477 (March 18, 2000).

Final Report explaining the April 20, 2000 amendments concerning multiple charges arising from a single criminal episode published with the Court's Order at 30 Pa.B. 2219 (May 6, 2000).

Final Report explaining the September 19, 2000 amendments clarifying the application of the rule to both summary and court cases published with the Court's Order at 30 Pa.B. 5135 (October 7, 2000).

Final Report explaining the May 10, 2002 amendments concerning advanced communication technology published with the Court's Order at 32 Pa.B. (May 25, 2002).

Final Report explaining the May 21, 2004 changes concerning joinder published with the Court's Order at 34 Pa.B. 2911 (June 5, 2004).

Source

The provisions of this Rule 130 amended April 20, 2000, effective July 1, 2000, 30 Pa.B. 2211; amended September 19, 2000, effective January 1, 2001, 30 Pa.B. 5135; amended May 10, 2002, effective September 1, 2002, 32 Pa.B. 2582; amended May 21, 2004, effective July 1, 2004, 34 Pa.B. 2910. Immediately preceding text appears at serial pages (289070) to (289072).

Rule 131. Location of Proceedings Before Issuing Authority.

(A) An issuing authority within the magisterial district for which he or she is elected or appointed shall have jurisdiction and authority to receive complaints,

1-24

issue warrants, hold preliminary arraignments, set and receive bail, issue commitments to jail, and hold hearings and summary trials.

(1)   Except as provided in paragraph (A)(2), all preliminary arraignments shall be held in the issuing authority's established office, a night court, or some other facility within the Commonwealth designated by the president judge, or the president judge's designee.

(2)   Preliminary arraignments may be conducted using advanced communication technology pursuant to Rule 540. The preliminary arraignment in these cases may be conducted from any site within the Commonwealth designated by the president judge, or the president judge's designee.

(3)   All hearings and summary trials before the issuing authority shall be held publicly at the issuing authority's established office. For reasons of emergency, security, size, or in the interests of justice, the president judge, or the president judge's designee, may order that a hearing or hearings, or a trial or trials, be held in another more suitable location within the judicial district.

(4)   The issuing authority may receive complaints, issue warrants, set and receive bail, and issue commitments to jail from any location within the judicial district, or from an advanced communication technology site within the Commonwealth.

(B)   When local conditions require, the president judge may establish procedures for preliminary hearings or summary trials, in all cases or in certain classes of cases, to be held at a central place or places within the judicial district at certain specified times. The procedures established shall provide either for the transfer of the case or the transfer of the issuing authority to the designated central place as the needs of justice and efficient administration require.

Comment

The 2002 amendments to paragraph (A) divided the paragraph into subparagraphs to more clearly distinguish between the locations for the different types of proceedings and business that an issuing authority conducts.

Paragraph (A)(3) permits the president judge, or the president judge's designee, to order that a hearing or hearings be held in a location that is different from the issuing authority's established office. Nothing in this rule is intended to preclude the president judge, or the president judge's designee, from issuing a standing order for a change in location. For example, this might be done when a state correctional institution is located in the judicial district and the president judge determines that, for security reasons, all preliminary hearings of the state correctional institution's inmates will be conducted at that prison.

See Rule 540 and Comment for the procedures governing the use of advanced communication technology in preliminary arraignments.

See Rule 130 concerning the venue when proceedings are conducted by using advanced communication technology.

Paragraph (B) of this rule is intended to facilitate compliance with the requirement that defendants be represented by counsel at the preliminary hearing. *Coleman v. Alabama*, 399 U. S. 1 (1970).

(312409) No. 370 Sep. 05

Paragraph (A)(4) permits issuing authorities to perform their official duties from an advanced communication technology site within the Commonwealth. The site may be located outside the magisterial district or judicial district where the issuing authority presides.

This rule allows the president judge of a judicial district the discretion to determine what classes of cases require centralized preliminary hearings or summary trials, and requires the president judge, or the president judge's designee, to establish a schedule of central places within the Commonwealth to conduct such hearings or summary trials, and the hours for the hearings or trials at the central locations.

Ideally, this rule should minimize the inconvenience to defense counsel and the attorney for the Commonwealth by eliminating the necessity of travel at various unpredictable times to many different locations throughout the judicial district for the purpose of attending preliminary hearings or summary trials. Finally, this rule allows preliminary hearings or summary trials for jailed defendants to be held at a location close to the place of detention.

Official Note: Formerly Rule 156, paragraph (a) adopted January 16, 1970, effective immediately; paragraph (a) amended and paragraph (b) adopted November 22, 1971, effective immediately; renumbered Rule 22 September 18, 1973, effective January 1, 1974; renumbered Rule 131 and amended March 1, 2000, effective April 1, 2001; amended March 12, 2002, effective July 1, 2002; amended May 10, 2002, effective September 1, 2002; amended June 30, 2005, effective August 1, 2006.

Committee Explanatory Reports:

Final Report explaining the March 1, 2000 reorganization and renumbering of the rules published with the Court's Order at 30 Pa.B. 1478 (March 18, 2000).

Final Report explaining the March 12, 2002 amendments concerning centralized courts for summary trials published with the Court's Order at 32 Pa.B. 1630 (March 30, 2002).

Final Report explaining the May 10, 2002 amendments concerning advanced communication technology published with the Court's Order at 32 Pa.B. 2591 (May 25, 2002).

Final Report explaining the June 30, 2005 deletion in paragraph (A) of "at all times" published with the Court's Order at 35 Pa.B. 3911 (July 16, 2005).

Source

The provisions of this Rule 131 amended March 12, 2002, effective July 1, 2002, 32 Pa.B. 1630; amended May 10, 2002, effective September 1, 2002, 32 Pa.B. 2582; amended June 30, 2005, effective August 1, 2006, 35 Pa.B. 3901. Immediately preceding text appears at serial pages (304106) and (289073) to (289074).

Rule 132. Temporary Assignment of Issuing Authorities.

(A) The president judge may assign temporarily the issuing authority of any magisterial district to serve another magisterial district whenever such assignment is needed:

    (1) to satisfy the requirements of Rule 117;

    (2) to insure fair and impartial proceedings;

1-26

(3) to conduct a preliminary hearing pursuant to Rule 544(B); or

(4) otherwise for the efficient administration of justice.

One or more issuing authorities may be so assigned to serve one or more magisterial districts.

(B) Whenever a temporary assignment is made under this rule, notice of such assignment shall be filed with the clerk of courts where it shall be available for police agencies and other interested persons.

(C) A motion may be filed requesting a temporary assignment under this rule on the ground that the assignment is needed to insure fair and impartial proceedings. Reasonable notice and opportunity to respond shall be provided to the parties.

(D) A motion shall be filed requesting a temporary assignment under paragraph (A)(3) whenever the attorney for the Commonwealth elects to proceed under Rule 544(B) following the refiling of a complaint.

Comment

The provisions of former paragraph (A) (Continuous Availability) were incorporated into new Rule 117 (Coverage: Issuing Warrants; Preliminary Arraignments and Summary Trials; and Setting and Accepting Bail) in 2005.

Paragraphs (A)(2) and (C) make explicit the authority of president judges to assign issuing authorities when necessary to insure fair and impartial proceedings, and to provide a procedure for a party to request such an assignment. Temporary assignment in this situation is intended to cover what might otherwise be referred to as "change of venue" at the magisterial district level. See, e.g., *Sufrich v. Commonwealth*, 68 Pa. Cmwlth. 42, 447 A.2d 1124 (1982).

The motion procedure of paragraph (C) is intended to apply when a party requests temporary assignment to insure fair and impartial proceedings. The president judge may, of course, order a response and schedule a hearing with regard to such a motion. However, this paragraph is not intended to require "a formal hearing ... beyond the narrow context of a motion for temporary assignment of issuing authority to insure fair and impartial proceedings predicated upon allegations which impugn the character or competence of the assigned issuing authority and which seek the recusal of the assigned issuing authority." See *Commonwealth v. Allem*, 367 Pa. Super. 173, 532 A.2d 845 (1987) (filing and service of the written motion and answer, and allowance of oral argument were more than adequate to meet the rule's requirements).

Paragraphs (A)(3) and (D) govern those situations in which the attorney for the Commonwealth, after refiling the complaint following the withdrawal or dismissal of any criminal charges at, or prior to, a preliminary hearing, determines that the preliminary hearing should be conducted by a different-issuing authority. See also Rule 544 (Reinstituting Charges Following Withdrawal or Dismissal). Under Rule 544, the president judge may designate another judge within the judicial district to handle reassignments.

The motion procedure is not intended to apply in any of the many other situations in which president judges make temporary assignments of issuing authorities; in all these other situations the president judges may make temporary assignments on their own without any motion, notice, response, or hearing.

Official Note: Formerly Rule 152, adopted January 16, 1970, effective immediately; amended and renumbered Rule 23 September 18, 1973, effective January 1, 1974; amended

October 21, 1983, effective January 1, 1984; amended February 27, 1995, effective July 1, 1995; amended October 8, 1999, effective January 1, 2000; renumbered Rule 132 and amended March 1, 2000, effective April 1, 2001; amended June 30, 2005, effective August 1, 2006.

Committee Explanatory Reports:

Final Report explaining the February 27, 1995 amendments published with the Court's Order at 25 Pa.B. 936 (March 18, 1995).

Final Report explaining the October 8, 1999 amendments concerning motions for temporary assignment of issuing authority following the reinstitution of criminal charges published with the Court's Order at 29 Pa.B. 5509 (October 23, 1999).

Final Report explaining the March 1, 2000 reorganization and renumbering of the rules published with the Court's Order at 30 Pa.B. 1478 (March 18, 2000).

Final Report explaining the June 30, 2005 changes to the rule correlative to the changes in procedure in new Rule 117 published with the Court's Order at 35 Pa.B. 3911 (July 16, 2005).

Source

The provisions of this Rule 132 amended June 30, 2005, effective July 1, 2006, 35 Pa.B. 3901. Immediately preceding text appears at serial pages (289074) to (289076).

Rule 133. Powers of Temporarily Assigned Issuing Authorities.

(A) Whenever an issuing authority is temporarily assigned to serve another magisterial district, the issuing authority shall, during the period of assignment, have the same jurisdiction and authority as one elected and qualified to serve in such magisterial district.

(B) An issuing authority so assigned may exercise such jurisdiction and authority in his or her own magisterial district or the magisterial district to which the issuing authority has been so assigned.

Official Note: Formerly Rule 153, adopted January 16, 1970, effective immediately; renumbered Rule 24 September 18, 1973, effective January 1, 1974 renumbered Rule 133 and amended March 1, 2000, effective April 1, 2001.

Committee Explanator Reports:

Final Report explaining the March 1, 2000 reorganization and renumbering of the rules published with the Court's Order at 30 Pa.B. 1477 (March 18, 2000).

Rule 134. Objections to Venue.

(A) Objections to venue between magisterial districts shall be raised in the court of common pleas of the judicial district in which the proceeding has been brought, before completion of the preliminary hearing in a court case or before completion of the summary trial when a summary offense is charged, or such objections shall be deemed to have been waived.

(B) No objection to venue between magisterial districts shall be allowed unless substantial prejudice will result if the proceeding is allowed to continue before the issuing authority before whom it has been brought.

(C) No criminal proceedings shall be dismissed because of improper venue between magisterial districts. Whenever an objection to such venue is allowed, the court of common pleas shall order the transfer of the proceeding to the issuing authority of the proper magisterial district.

Comment

An objection to venue under this rule would include a challenge to the transfer of proceedings pursuant to Rule 130(B).

Official Note: Formerly Rule 155, adopted January 6, 1970, effective immediately; renumbered Rule 25 September 18, 1973, effective January 16, 1974; amended January 28, 1983, effective July 1, 1983; renumbered Rule 134 and amended March 1, 2000, effective April 1, 2001; amended April 20, 2000, effective July 1, 2000.

Committee Explanatory Reports:

Final Report explaining the March 1, 2000 reorganization and renumbering of the rules published with the Court's Order at 30 Pa.B. 1477 (March 18, 2000).

Final Report explaining the April 20, 2000 amendments concerning multiple charges arising from a single criminal episode published with the Court's Order at 30 Pa.B. 2219 (May 6, 2000).

Source

The provisions of this Rule 134 amended April 20, 2000, effective July 1, 2000, 30 Pa.B. 2211. Immediately preceding text appears at serial page (264132).

Rule 135. Transcript of Proceedings Before Issuing Authority.

(A)   The issuing authority shall prepare and forward to the court of common pleas a transcript of the proceedings in all summary cases when an appeal is taken and in all court cases when the defendant is held for court.

(B)   The transcript shall contain the following information, where applicable;

(1)   the date and place of hearings;

(2)   the names and addresses of the prosecutor, defendant, and witnesses;

(3)   the names and office addresses of counsel in the proceeding;

(4)   the charge against the defendant as set forth in the prosecutor's complaint;

(5)   the date of issuance of any citation, summons, or warrant of arrest and the return of service thereon;

(6)   a statement whether the parties and witnesses were sworn and which of these persons testified;

(7)   when the defendant was held for court the amount of bail set;

(8)   the nature of the bail posted and the name and address of the corporate surety or individual surety;

(9)   a notation that the defendant has or has not been fingerprinted;

(10)   a specific description of any defect properly raised in accordance with Rule 109;

(11)   a notation that the defendant was advised of the right to apply for the assignment of counsel;

(12)   the defendant's plea of guilty or not guilty, the decision that was rendered in the case and the date thereof, and the judgment of sentence and place of confinement, if any;

1-27

(13) any other information required by the rules to be in the issuing authority's transcript.

Comment

The requirement of a docket was deleted from this rule in 1985 because dockets are now routinely maintained under the supervision of the Administrative Office of Pennsylvania Courts. It is expected that issuing authorities will continue to keep dockets of criminal proceedings. The transcript requirements presuppose an accurate docket to supply the information necessary to prepare a transcript.

The procedures regarding the filing of a transcript after appeal in summary cases are set forth in Rule 460(C) and (D). For such procedures after the defendant is held for court in a court case, see Rule 547. With regard to other information required by the rules to be in the transcript, see, e.g. Rule 542.

The requirement that there be a notation indicating whether the defendant has been fingerprinted as required by the Criminal History Record Information Act, 18 Pa.C.S. § 9112, is to alert the district attorney and the court whether it is necessary to have the defendant fingerprinted after the case is held for court.

Official Note: Formerly Rule 125 adopted June 30, 1964, effective January 1, 1965; suspended effective May 1, 1970, revised January 31, 1970, effective May 1, 1970; renumbered Rule 26 and subparagraphs (b)(5) and (b)(10) amended September 18, 1973, effective January 1, 1974; subparagraph (b)(10) amended April 8, 1982, effective July 1, 1982; previous subparagraph (b)(7) deleted January 28, 1983, effective July 1, 1983; amended July 12, 1985, effective January 1, 1986; effective date extended to July 1, 1986; renumbered Rule 135 and amended March 1, 2000, effective April 1, 2001; amended July 10, 2008, effective February 1, 2009.

Committee Explanatory Reports:

Final Report explaining the March 1, 2000 reorganization and renumbering of the rules published with the Court's Order at 30 Pa.B. 1477 (March 18, 2000).

Final Report explaining the July 10, 2008 amendment adding new paragraph (9) requiring a notation of fingerprinting published with the Courts Order at 38 Pa.B. 3975 (July 26, 2008).

Source

The provisions of this Rule 135 amended July 10, 2008, effective February 1, 2009, 38 Pa.B. 3971. Immediately preceding text appears at serial pages (312413) and (264133).

PART D. Procedures Implementing 42 Pa.C.S. §§ 4137, 4138, and 4139: Criminal Contempt Powers of District Justices, Judges of the Pittsburgh Magistrates Court, and Judges of the Traffic Court of Philadelphia

Rule 140. Contempt Proceedings Before Magisterial District Judges, Pittsburgh Magistrates Court Judges, and Philadelphia Traffic Court Judges.

(A) CONTEMPT IN THE PRESENCE OF THE COURT

1. An issuing authority may summarily hold an individual in contempt for misbehavior in the presence of the court that obstructs the administration of justice, and, after affording the individual an opportunity to be heard, may impose a punishment of a fine of not more than $100 or imprisonment for not more than 30 days or both.

1-28

2. The issuing authority shall orally advise the contemnor of the right to appeal within 30 days for a trial *de novo* in the court of common pleas, and that:

    a. any punishment shall be automatically stayed for a period of 30 days from the date of the imposition of the punishment;

    b. if the contemnor files an appeal within the 30-day period, the stay will remain in effect pending disposition of the appeal;

    c. when the punishment is imprisonment, the contemnor has the right to assistance of counsel for the purpose of the *de novo* hearing in the court of common pleas, and, if the contemnor is without financial resources or otherwise unable to employ counsel, counsel will be assigned as provided in Rule 122;

    d. the contemnor must appear in the court of common pleas for the *de novo* hearing or the appeal may be dismissed; and

    e. unless a notice of appeal is filed within the 30-day period, on the date specified by the issuing authority, the contemnor must:

        (1)   pay any fine imposed; and

        (2)   appear before the issuing authority for execution of any punishment of imprisonment.

3. The issuing authority shall issue a written order of contempt, in which the issuing authority shall:

    a. set forth the facts of the case that constitute the contempt;

    b. certify that the issuing authority saw or heard the conduct constituting the contempt, and that the contempt was committed in the actual presence of the issuing authority;

    c. set forth the punishment imposed, and the date on which the contemnor is to pay any fine or to appear for the execution of any punishment of imprisonment; and

    d. set forth the information specified in paragraph (A)2.

4. The order of contempt shall be signed by the issuing authority, and a copy shall be given to the contemnor.

(B) CONTEMPT NOT IN THE PRESENCE OF THE COURT

  1. INSTITUTION OF PROCEEDINGS

    a. An issuing authority may institute contempt proceedings by either

        (1)   giving written notice to the alleged contemnor of the time, date, and place of the contempt hearing, or

        (2)   when deemed appropriate by the issuing authority, issuing an attachment by means of a warrant,

whenever a person is alleged to have (i) failed to obey a subpoena issued by the issuing authority; (ii) failed to comply with an order of the issuing authority directing a defendant to pay fines and costs in accordance with an installment payment order; (iii) failed to comply with an order of an issuing authority directing a defendant to compensate a victim; or (iv) failed to

1-29

comply with an order of an issuing authority in any case in which the issuing authority is by statute given the power to find the person in contempt.

b. If the proceedings are instituted by notice, the notice shall:

(1)   specify the acts or omissions and the essential facts constituting the contempt charged;

(2)   advise what the punishment may be for a finding of contempt in the case;

(3)   if, in the event of a finding of contempt, there is a likelihood that the punishment will be imprisonment, advise the alleged contemnor of the right to the assistance of counsel and that counsel will be assigned pursuant to Rule 122 if the alleged contemnor is without financial resources or is otherwise unable to employ counsel; and

(4)   advise the alleged contemnor that failure to appear at the hearing may result in the issuance of a bench warrant.

c. The notice shall be served in person or by both first class and certified mail, return receipt requested.

2. HEARING

a. The hearing shall be conducted in open court, and the alleged contemnor shall be given a reasonable opportunity to defend.

b. At the conclusion of the hearing:

(1)   The issuing authority in open court shall announce the decision, and, upon a finding of contempt, impose punishment, if any.

(2)   If the issuing authority finds contempt and imposes punishment, the issuing authority shall orally advise the contemnor of the right to appeal within 30 days for a trial *de novo* in the court of common pleas, and that:

(a)   any punishment shall be automatically stayed for a period of 30 days from the date of the imposition of the punishment;

(b)   if the contemnor files an appeal within the 30-day period, the stay will remain in effect until disposition of the appeal;

(c)   when the punishment is imprisonment, that the contemnor has the right to assistance of counsel for the purpose of the *de novo* hearing in the court of common pleas and, if the contemnor is without financial resources or otherwise unable to employ counsel, that counsel will be assigned as provided in Rule 122;

(d)   the contemnor must appear in the court of common pleas for the *de novo* hearing or the appeal may be dismissed; and

(e)   unless a notice of appeal is filed within the 30-day period, on the date specified by the issuing authority, the contemnor must:

(i)   pay any fine imposed; and

(ii)   appear before the issuing authority for execution of any punishment of imprisonment.

(372106) No. 477 Aug. 14

(3)   If the issuing authority finds contempt and imposes punishment, the issuing authority shall issue a written order of contempt setting forth:

(a)   the facts of the case that constitute the contempt;

(b)   the punishment imposed, and the date on which the contemnor is to pay any fine or to appear for the execution of any punishment of imprisonment; and

(c)   the information specified in paragraph (B)2.b(2).

(4)   The order of contempt shall be signed by the issuing authority, and a copy given to the contemnor.

(5)   Whether or not the issuing authority finds an individual in contempt for failure to comply with an order to pay restitution or to pay fines and costs, the issuing authority may alter or amend the order. If the issuing authority alters or amends the order, the issuing authority shall:

(a)   issue a written order setting forth the amendments and the reasons for the amendments, make the order a part of the transcript, and give a copy of the order to the defendant; and

(b)   advise the defendant that the defendant has 30 days within which to file a notice of appeal of the altered or amended order pursuant to Rule 141.

c. The issuing authority shall not hold a contempt hearing in the absence of the alleged contemnor. If the alleged contemnor fails to appear for the contempt hearing, the issuing authority may continue the hearing and issue a bench warrant.

3. PUNISHMENT

Punishment for contempt may not exceed the limits set forth as follows:

a. Whenever a person is found to have failed to obey a subpoena issued by the issuing authority, punishment may be a fine of not more than $100. Failure to pay the fine within a reasonable time may result in imprisonment for not more than 10 days.

b. Whenever a person is found to have failed to comply with an order of the issuing authority directing a defendant to pay fines and costs in accordance with an installment payment order, punishment may be imprisonment for not more than 90 days.

c. Whenever a person is found to have failed to comply with an order of an issuing authority directing a defendant to compensate a victim, punishment may be a fine of not more than $100 or imprisonment for not more than 30 days, or both.

Comment

This rule sets forth the procedures to implement 42 Pa.C.S. §§ 4137, 4138, and 4139 concerning contempt powers of the minor judiciary, as well as any other statutes subsequently enacted that would provide for findings of contempt by the minor judiciary. It is not intended to supplant the procedures set forth in 23 Pa.C.S. § 6110 *et seq.* concerning violations of protection from abuse orders.

1-31

The scope of the contempt powers of magisterial district judges, Pittsburgh Magistrates Court judges, and Philadelphia Traffic Court judges is governed by 42 Pa.C.S. §§ 4137, 4138, and 4139 respectively. Therefore, as used in this rule, "issuing authority" refers only to magisterial district judges, Pittsburgh Magistrates Court judges, and Philadelphia Traffic Court judges when acting within the scope of their contempt powers. However, 42 Pa.C.S. §§ 4137(c), 4138(c), and 4139(c) contain limitations upon the punishment that a minor court may impose for contempt. Such statutory limitations were held to be unconstitutional in *Commonwealth v. McMullen*, 599 Pa. 435, 961 A.2d 842 (2008).

By Orders dated November 29, 2004, 34 Pa.B. 6507 (December 11, 2004) and February 25, 2005, 35 Pa.B. 1662 (March 12, 2005), the Pennsylvania Supreme Court created an administrative judicial unit referred to as the Pittsburgh Municipal Court and assigned all matters within the jurisdiction of the Pittsburgh Magistrates Court to the Pittsburgh Municipal Court. As a result of these orders, the Pittsburgh Magistrates Court is no longer staffed while the Pittsburgh Municipal Court is staffed by Allegheny County magisterial district judges assigned on a rotating basis. The terminology is retained in these rules because the Pittsburgh Magistrates Court, which is created by statute, has not been disestablished by the statute.

Pursuant to Act 17 of 2013, P. L. 55, No. 17 (June 19, 2013), the jurisdiction and functions of the Philadelphia Traffic Court were transferred to the Philadelphia Municipal Court Traffic Division. The terminology is retained in these rules because the Philadelphia Traffic Court, which is created by the Pennsylvania Constitution, has not been disestablished by constitutional amendment. Hearing officers of the Philadelphia Municipal Court Traffic Division do not have contempt powers of Philadelphia Traffic Court judges under 42 Pa.C.S. § 4139.

All contempt proceedings under this rule are to be entered on the issuing authority's miscellaneous docket, and a separate docket transcript for the contempt proceeding is to be prepared. If an appeal is taken, the issuing authority is required to forward the transcript and the contempt order to the clerk of courts. *See* Rule 141.

Paragraph (A) sets forth the procedures for handling contempt proceedings when the misbehavior is committed in the presence of the court and is obstructing the administration of justice. *See* 42 Pa.C.S. §§ 4137(a)(1), 4138(a)(1), and 4139(a)(1). This type of contempt is commonly referred to as "direct" or "summary" contempt. The issuing authority may immediately impose punishment without a formal hearing because prompt action is necessary to maintain or restore order in the courtroom and to protect the authority and dignity of the court. Although immediate action is permitted in these cases, the alleged contemnor is ordinarily given an opportunity to be heard before the imposition of punishment. *See Commonwealth v. Stevenson*, 482 Pa. 76, 393 A.2d 386 (1978).

Customarily, individuals are not held in summary contempt for misbehavior before the court without prior oral warning by the presiding judicial officer.

Paragraph (B) provides the procedures for instituting and conducting proceedings in all other cases of alleged contemptuous conduct subject to the minor judiciary's statutory contempt powers, which are commonly referred to as "indirect criminal contempt" proceedings.

For purposes of this rule, the phrase "failed to obey a subpoena issued by the issuing authority" in paragraph (B)(1)(a) is intended to include the failure to obey any other lawful process ordering the person to appear before an issuing authority.

Pursuant to 42 Pa.C.S. §§ 4137(a)(2), (3), and (4), 4138(a)(2) and (3), and 4139(a)(2) and (3), only issuing authorities have the power to impose punishment for contempt of court for failure to comply with an order directing a defendant to compensate a victim. *See* paragraph (B)1.a.

"Indirect criminal contempt" proceedings must be instituted either by serving the alleged contemnor with a notice of the contempt hearing, or by issuing an attachment in the form of a warrant. The alleged contemnor must be afforded the same due process protections that are normally provided in

1-32

Copyright © 2014 Commonwealth of Pennsylvania

criminal proceedings, including notice of the charges, an opportunity to be heard and to present a defense, and counsel. *See, e.g., Codispoti v. Pennsylvania*, 418 U. S. 506 (1974), and *Bloom v. Illinois*, 391 U. S. 194 (1968).

When a warrant is executed under this rule, the alleged contemnor should be taken without unreasonable delay before the proper issuing authority.

Although 42 Pa.C.S. §§ 4137(a)(4), 4138(a)(3), and 4139(a)(3) permit an issuing authority to impose summary punishments for indirect criminal contempt when a defendant fails to comply with an order of the issuing authority directing the defendant to pay fines and costs in accordance with an installment payment order, nothing in this rule is intended to preclude an issuing authority from proceeding pursuant to Rule 456 (Default Procedures: Restitution, Fines, and Costs).

No defendant may be sentenced to imprisonment if the right to counsel was not afforded at the contempt hearing. *See Alabama v. Shelton*, 535 U. S. 654 (2002), *Scott v. Illinois*, 440 U. S. 367 (1979), and *Argersinger v. Hamlin*, 407 U. S. 25 (1972). *Also see* Rule 454 concerning counsel in summary cases. The Supreme Court in *Commonwealth v. Abrams*, 461 Pa. 327, 336 A.2d 308 (1975) held that the right to counsel applies in cases of criminal contempt. *See also Commonwealth v. Crawford*, 466 Pa. 269, 352 A.2d 52 (1976).

For the assignment of counsel, follow the Rule 122 procedures for summary cases.

For waiver of counsel, follow the Rule 121 procedures for proceedings before an issuing authority.

For the procedures for taking, perfecting, and handling an appeal from an order entered pursuant to this rule, see Rule 141.

If a contemnor defaults in the payment of a fine imposed as punishment for contempt pursuant to this rule, the matter is to proceed as provided in Rule 142.

See Chapter 5 Part C concerning bail before a contempt hearing. *See* 42 Pa.C.S. § 4137(e) concerning a magisterial district judge's authority to set bail after an adjudication of contempt.

Paragraphs (A)2.e and (B)2.b(2)(e) require the issuing authority to set a date for the contemnor to pay any fine or to appear for execution of any punishment of imprisonment. This date should be at least 35 days from the date of the contempt proceeding to allow for the expiration of the 30-day automatic stay period and the 5-day period within which the clerk of courts is to serve a copy of the notice of appeal on the issuing authority. *See* Rule 141.

Paragraph (B)2.b(5) requires that the case be reviewed at the conclusion of a contempt hearing to determine whether the restitution order or the fines and costs installment order should be altered or amended, rather than scheduling another hearing. This review should be conducted whether or not the issuing authority finds an individual in contempt for failure to comply with an order to pay restitution, or whether or not the issuing authority finds an individual in contempt for failure to comply with an installment order to pay fines and costs. For the authority to alter or amend a restitution order, see 18 Pa.C.S. § 1106(c)(3).

Official Note: Rule 30 adopted October 1, 1997, effective October 1, 1998; renumbered Rule 140 and amended March 1, 2000, effective April 1, 2001; Comment revised March 26, 2004, effective July 1, 2004; amended March 1, 2012, effective July 1, 2012; Comment revised May 7, 2014, effective immediately.

Committee Explanatory Reports:

Final Report explaining the provisions of new Rule 30 published with the Court's Order at 27 Pa.B. 5405 (October 18, 1997).

Final Report explaining the March 1, 2000 reorganization and renumbering of the rules published with the Court's Order at 30 Pa.B. 1478 (March 18, 2000).

Final Report explaining the March 26, 2004 Comment revision concerning right to counsel published with the Court's Order at 34 Pa.B. 1931 (April 10, 2004).

Final Report explaining the March 1, 2012 amendments concerning limitations on punishment for contempt published with the Court's Order at 42 Pa.B. 1367 (March 17, 2012).

Final Report explaining the May 7, 2014 Comment revision concerning the transfer of the Philadelphia Traffic Court functions to the Philadelphia Municipal Court published with the Court's Order at 44 Pa.B. 3065 (May 24, 2014).

Source

The provisions of this Rule 140 amended March 26, 2004, effective July 1, 2004, 34 Pa.B. 1929; amended March 1, 2012, effective July 1, 2012, 42 Pa.B. 1364; amended May 7, 2014, effective immediately, 44 Pa.B. 3056. Immediately preceeding text appears at serial pages (360830) to (360835).

Rule 141. Appeals from Contempt Adjudications by Magisterial District Judges, Pittsburgh Magistrates Court Judges, or Philadelphia Traffic Court Judges.

(A) An appeal authorized by 42 Pa.C.S. §§ 4137(d), 4138(d), or 4139(d) of the action of an issuing authority in a contempt proceeding shall be perfected by filing a notice of appeal within 30 days after the action of the issuing authority with the clerk of courts and by appearing in the court of common pleas for the *de novo* hearing.

(B) In all cases, the punishment imposed for contempt shall be stayed for 30 days from the imposition of the punishment. If an appeal is filed within the 30-day period, the stay shall remain in effect pending disposition of the appeal.

(C) The notice of appeal shall contain the following information:

    (1) the name and address of the appellant;

    (2) the name and address of the issuing authority who heard the case;

    (3) the magisterial district number where the case was heard;

    (4) the date of the imposition of punishment;

    (5) the punishment imposed;

    (6) the type or amount of bail furnished to the issuing authority, if any; and

    (7) the name and address of the attorney, if any, filing the notice of appeal.

(D) Within 5 days after the filing of the notice of appeal, the clerk of courts shall serve a copy either personally or by mail upon the issuing authority.

(E) The issuing authority shall, within 20 days after receipt of the notice of appeal, file with the clerk of courts:

    (1) the transcript of the proceedings;

    (2) either the notice of the hearing or a copy of the attachment;

    (3) the contempt order; and

    (4) any bench warrant.

(F) Upon the filing of the transcript and other papers by the issuing authority, the case shall be heard *de novo* by the appropriate division of the court of common pleas as the president judge shall direct.

    (1) If the judge assigned to hear the matter finds contempt and imposes punishment, the case shall remain in the court of common pleas for execution of any punishment, including the collection of any fines or costs.

1-34

(2) If the appellant fails to appear for the *de novo* hearing, the judge may dismiss the appeal and enter judgment in the court of common pleas on the judgment of the issuing authority.

(3) If the appellant withdraws the appeal, the judge may dismiss the appeal and enter judgment in the court of common pleas on the judgment of the issuing authority.

Comment

This rule provides the procedures for taking an appeal from a finding of contempt by a magisterial district judge, a Pittsburgh Magistrates Court judge, or a Philadelphia Traffic Court judge.

As used in this rule, "issuing authority" refers only to magisterial district judges, Pittsburgh Magistrates Court judges, and Philadelphia Traffic Court judges when acting within the scope of their contempt powers. *See* 42 Pa.C.S. §§ 4137, 4138, and 4139.

By Orders dated November 29, 2004, 34 Pa.B. 6507 (December 11, 2004) and February 25, 2005, 35 Pa.B. 1662 (March 12, 2005), the Pennsylvania Supreme Court created an administrative judicial unit referred to as the Pittsburgh Municipal Court and assigned all matters within the jurisdiction of the Pittsburgh Magistrates Court to the Pittsburgh Municipal Court. As a result of these orders, the Pittsburgh Magistrates Court is no longer staffed while the Pittsburgh Municipal Court is staffed by Allegheny County magisterial district judges assigned on a rotating basis. The terminology is retained in these rules because the Pittsburgh Magistrates Court, which is created by statute, has not been disestablished by the statute.

Pursuant to Act 17 of 2013, P. L. 55, No. 17 (June 19, 2013), the jurisdiction and functions of the Philadelphia Traffic Court were transferred to the Philadelphia Municipal Court Traffic Division. The terminology is retained in these rules because the Philadelphia Traffic Court, which is created by the Pennsylvania Constitution, has not been disestablished by constitutional amendment. Hearing officers of the Philadelphia Municipal Court Traffic Division do not have contempt powers of Philadelphia Traffic Court judges under 42 Pa.C.S. § 4139.

As the Pennsylvania Supreme Court stated in *Commonwealth v. McMullen*, 599 Pa. 435, 961 A.2d 842 (2008), legislative limitations on a court's power to sentence for contempt are unconstitutional.

Pursuant to paragraph (B), any punishment imposed for contempt will be automatically stayed for 30 days from the date of the imposition of the punishment, during which time a notice of appeal may be filed with the clerk of courts. To the extent that 42 Pa.C.S. §§ 4137(d), 4138(d), and 4139(d) are inconsistent with this rule, they are suspended by Rule 1101 (Suspension of Acts of Assembly).

If no notice of appeal is filed within the 30-day period following imposition of the punishment, Rule 140 requires the issuing authority to direct the contemnor on a date certain to pay any fine imposed or to appear for execution of any punishment of imprisonment.

See 42 Pa.C.S. § 4137(e) concerning the imposition of bail as a condition of release by a magisterial district judge.

The procedures set forth in Rule 462 (Trial *De Novo*) for a trial *de novo* on a summary case should be followed when a contempt adjudication is appealed to the common pleas court.

No defendant may be sentenced to imprisonment if the right to counsel was not afforded at the de novo contempt hearing *See Alabama v. Shelton*, 535 U. S. 654 (2002), *Scott v. Illinois*, 440 U. S. 367 (1979), and *Argersinger v. Hamlin*, 407 U. S. 25 (1972).

Paragraph (F) makes it clear that the judge assigned to conduct the de novo hearing may dismiss an appeal of the action of an issuing authority in a contempt proceeding when the judge determines that the appellant is absent without cause from the *de novo* hearing. If the appeal is dismissed, the judge should enter judgment and order execution of any punishment imposed by the issuing authority.

Once punishment for a contempt adjudication is imposed, paragraph (F)(1) makes it clear that the case is to remain in the court of common pleas for execution of the sentence and collection of any fine and costs, and the case may not be returned to the issuing authority.

Official Note: Rule 31 adopted October 1, 1997, effective October 1, 1998; renumbered Rule 141 and Comment revised March 1, 2000, effective April 1, 2001; amended February 28, 2003, effective July 1, 2003; Comment revised March 26, 2004, effective July 1, 2004; amended March 1, 2012, effective July 1, 2012; Comment revised May 7, 2014, effective immediately.

Committee Explanatory Reports:

Final Report explaining the provisions of new Rule 31 published with the Court's Order at 27 Pa.B. 5405 (October 18, 1997).

Final Report explaining the March 1, 2000 reorganization and renumbering of the rules published with the Court's Order at 30 Pa.B. 1478 (March 18, 2000).

Final Report explaining the February 28, 2003 amendments concerning contempt appeals published with the Court's Order at 33 Pa.B. 1326 (March 15, 2003).

Final Report explaining the March 26, 2004 Comment revision concerning right to counsel published with the Court's Order at 34 Pa.B. 1931 (April 10, 2004).

Final Report explaining the March 1, 2012 amendments regarding limitations on punishment for contempt published with the Court's Order at 42 Pa.B. 1367 (March 17, 2012).

Final Report explaining the May 7, 2014 Comment revision concerning the transfer of the Philadelphia Traffic Court functions to the Philadelphia Municipal Court published with the Court's Order at 44 Pa.B. 3065 (May 24, 2014).

Source

The provisions of this Rule 141 amended February 28, 2003, effective July 1, 2003, 33 Pa.B. 1324; amended March 26, 2004, effective July 1, 2004, 34 Pa.B. 1929; amended March 1, 2012, effective July 1, 2012, 42 Pa.B. 1364; amended May 7, 2014, effective immediately, 44 Pa.B. 3056. Immediately preceding text appears at serial pages (360836) to (360838).

Rule 142. Procedures Governing Defaults in Payment of Fine Imposed as Punishment for Contempt.

(A) If a contemnor defaults on the payment of a fine imposed as punishment for contempt pursuant to Rule 140(A)(1) and (B)(3), the issuing authority shall notify the contemnor in person or by first class mail that within 10 days of the date on the default notice the contemnor must either:

(1) pay the amount due as ordered, or

(2) appear before the issuing authority to explain why the contemnor should not be imprisoned for nonpayment as provided by law, or a bench warrant for the contemnor's arrest shall be issued.

(B) When the contemnor appears either in response to the paragraph (A)(2) notice or following an arrest with a warrant issued pursuant to paragraph (A), the issuing authority shall conduct a hearing to determine whether the contemnor is financially able to pay as ordered.

(1) Upon a determination that the defendant is financially able to pay as ordered, the issuing authority may impose imprisonment for nonpayment, as provided by law.

1-36

(2)   Upon a determination that the contemnor is financially unable to pay as ordered, the issuing authority may order a schedule for installment payments.

(C)   A contemnor may appeal an issuing authority's determination pursuant to this rule by filing a notice of appeal within 30 days of the issuing authority's order. The appeal shall proceed as provided in Rule 141.

Comment

This rule provides the procedures governing defaults in the payment of fines imposed as punishment for contempt in proceedings before magisterial district judges, Pittsburgh Magistrates Court judges, and Philadelphia Traffic Court judges. *See* Rule 140(A)(1) and (B)(3).

As used in this rule, "issuing authority" refers only to magisterial district judges, Pittsburgh Magistrates Court judges, and Philadelphia Traffic Court judges when acting within the scope of their contempt powers. *See* 42 Pa.C.S. §§ 4137, 4138, and 4139.

By Orders dated November 29, 2004, 34 Pa.B. 6507 (December 11, 2004) and February 25, 2005, 35 Pa.B. 1662 (March 12, 2005), the Pennsylvania Supreme Court created an administrative judicial unit referred to as the Pittsburgh Municipal Court and assigned all matters within the jurisdiction of the Pittsburgh Magistrates Court to the Pittsburgh Municipal Court. As a result of these orders, the Pittsburgh Magistrates Court is no longer staffed while the Pittsburgh Municipal Court is staffed by Allegheny County magisterial district judges assigned on a rotating basis. The terminology is retained in these rules because the Pittsburgh Magistrates Court, which is created by statute, has not been disestablished by the statute.

Pursuant to Act 17 of 2013, P. L. 55, No. 17 (June 19, 2013), the jurisdiction and functions of the Philadelphia Traffic Court were transferred to the Philadelphia Municipal Court Traffic Division. The terminology is retained in these rules because the Philadelphia Traffic Court, which is created by the Pennsylvania Constitution, has not been disestablished by constitutional amendment. Hearing officers of the Philadelphia Municipal Court Traffic Division do not have contempt powers of Philadelphia Traffic Court judges under 42 Pa.C.S. § 4139.

For contempt procedures generally, see Rule 140.

As the Pennsylvania Supreme Court stated in *Commonwealth v. McMullen*, 599 Pa. 435, 961 A.2d 842 (2008), legislative limitations on a court's power to sentence for contempt are unconstitutional.

When a contemnor defaults on a payment of a fine, paragraph (A) requires the issuing authority to notify the contemnor of the default, and to provide the contemnor with an opportunity to either pay the amount due or appear within a 10-day period to explain why the contemnor should not be imprisoned for nonpayment. If the contemnor fails to pay or appear, the issuing authority must issue a bench warrant for the arrest of the contemnor.

If the hearing on the default cannot be held immediately, the issuing authority may set bail as provided in Chapter 5 Part C.

This rule contemplates that when there has been an appeal pursuant to paragraph (C), the case would return to the issuing authority who presided at the default hearing for completion of the collection process.

Official Note: Rule 32 adopted October 1, 1997, effective October 1, 1998; renumbered Rule 142 and amended March 1, 2000, effective April 1, 2001; amended March 3, 2004, effective July 1, 2004; amended March 1, 2012, effective July 1, 2012; Comment revised May 7, 2014, effective immediately.

1-37

Committee Explanatory Reports:

Final Report explaining the provisions of new Rule 32 published with the Court's Order at 27 Pa.B. 5405 (October 18, 1997).

Final Report explaining the March 1, 2000 reorganization and renumbering of the rules published with the Court's Order at 30 Pa.B. 1478 (March 18, 2000).

Final Report explaining the March 3, 2004 rule changes deleting "show cause" published with the Court's Order at 34 Pa.B. 1561 (March 20, 2004).

Final Report explaining the March 1, 2012 rule changes regarding limitations on punishment for contempt published with the Court's Order at 42 Pa.B. 1367 (March 17, 2012).

Final Report explaining the May 7, 2014 Comment revision concerning the transfer of the Philadelphia Traffic Court functions to the Philadelphia Municipal Court published with the Court's Order at 44 Pa.B. 3065 (May 24, 2014).

Source

The provisions of this Rule 142 amended March 3, 2004, effective July 1, 2004, 34 Pa.B. 1547; amended March 1, 2012, effective July 1, 2012, 42 Pa.B. 1364; amended May 7, 2014, effective immediately, 44 Pa.B. 3056. Immediately preceeding text appears at serial pages (360838) and (369627).

PART E. Miscellaneous Warrants

Rule 150. Bench Warrants.

(A) In a court case when a bench warrant is executed, the case is to proceed in accordance with the following procedures.

(1) When a defendant or witness is arrested pursuant to a bench warrant, he or she shall be taken without unnecessary delay for a hearing on the bench warrant. The hearing shall be conducted by the judicial officer who issued the bench warrant, or, another judicial officer designated by the president judge or by the president judge's designee to conduct bench warrant hearings.

(2) In the discretion of the judicial officer, the bench warrant hearing may be conducted using two-way simultaneous audio-visual communication.

(3) When the individual is arrested in the county of issuance, if the bench warrant hearing cannot be conducted promptly after the arrest, the defendant or witness shall be lodged in the county jail pending the hearing. The authority in charge of the county jail promptly shall notify the court that the individual is being held pursuant to the bench warrant.

(4) When the individual is arrested outside the county of issuance, the authority in charge of the county jail promptly shall notify the proper authorities in the county of issuance that the individual is being held pursuant to the bench warrant.

(5) The bench warrant hearing shall be conducted without unnecessary delay after the individual is lodged in the jail of the county of issuance on that bench warrant.

(a)   When the bench warrant is issued by the supervising judge of a "multi-county" investigating grand jury, the individual shall be detained only until the supervising judge is available to conduct the bench warrant hearing.

(b)   In all other cases, the individual shall not be detained without a bench warrant hearing on that bench warrant longer than 72 hours, or the close of the next business day if the 72 hours expires on a non-business day.

(6)   At the conclusion of the bench warrant hearing following the disposition of the matter, the judicial officer immediately shall vacate the bench warrant.

(7)   If a bench warrant hearing is not held within the time limits in paragraph (A)(5)(b), the bench warrant shall expire by operation of law.

(B)   As used in this rule, "judicial officer" is limited to the magisterial district judge or common pleas court judge who issued the bench warrant, or the magisterial district judge or common pleas court judge designated by the president judge or by the president judge's designee to conduct bench warrant hearings, or in Philadelphia, trial commissioners.

Comment

This rule addresses only the procedures to be followed after a bench warrant is executed, and does not apply to execution of bench warrants outside the Commonwealth, which are governed by the extradition procedures in 42 Pa.C.S. § 9101 *et seq.*, or to warrants issued in connection with probation or parole proceedings.

For the bench warrant procedures when a witness is under the age of 18 years, see Rule 151.

Paragraph (A)(2) permits the bench warrant hearing to be conducted using two-way simultaneous audio-visual communication, which is a form of advanced communication technology. *See* Rule 103. Utilizing this technology will aid the court in complying with this rule, and in ensuring individuals arrested on bench warrants are not detained unnecessarily.

Once a bench warrant is executed and the defendant is taken into custody, the bench warrant no longer is valid.

To ensure compliance with the prompt bench warrant hearing requirement, the president judge or the president judge's designee may designate only a magisterial district judge to cover for magisterial district judges or a common pleas court judge to cover for common pleas court judges. *See also* Rule

(372115) No. 477 Aug. 14

1-38.2

132 for the temporary assignment of magisterial district judges. In Philadelphia, the current practice of designating trial commissioners to conduct bench warrant hearings is acknowledged in paragraph (B).

It is expected that the practices in some judicial districts of a common pleas court judge (1) indicating on a bench warrant the judge has issued that the bench warrant is a "judge only" bench warrant, or (2) who knows he or she will be unavailable asking another common pleas court judge to handle his or her cases during the common pleas court judge's absence, would continue.

Paragraph (A)(5)(a) recognizes the procedural and substantive differences between "multi-county" investigating grand jury proceedings and all other proceedings in the court of common pleas, including a county investigating grand jury, by eliminating the time limit for conducting the bench warrant hearing when the bench warrant is issued by the multi-county investigating grand jury supervising judge. *See* Rules 240—244 and 42 Pa.C.S. § 4544. When the supervising judge issues a bench warrant, the bench warrant hearing must be conducted expeditiously when the supervising judge is available.

Paragraph (A)(6) requires the judicial officer to vacate the bench warrant at the conclusion of the bench warrant hearing. The current practice in some judicial districts of having the clerk of courts cancel the bench warrant upon receipt of a return of service is consistent with this paragraph, as long as the clerk of courts promptly provides notice of the return of service to the issuing judge.

It is incumbent upon the president judge or the president judge's designee to establish procedures for the monitoring of the time individuals are detained pending their bench warrant hearing.

For the procedures concerning violation of the conditions of bail, see Chapter 5 Part C.

As used in this rule, "court" includes magisterial district judge courts.

For the bench warrant procedures in summary cases, see Rules 430(B) and 431(C).

For the arrest warrants that initiate proceedings in court cases, see Chapter 5, Part B(3)(a), Rules 513, 514, 515, 516, 517, and 518. For the arrest warrants that initiate proceedings in summary cases, see Chapter 4, Part D(1), Rules 430(A) and 431(B).

Official Note: Adopted December 30, 2005, effective August 1, 2006; Comment revised October 24, 2013, effective January 1, 2014.

Committee Explanatory Reports:

Final Report explaining new Rule 150 providing procedures for bench warrants published with the Court's Order at 36 Pa.B. 184 (January 14, 2006).

Final Report explaining the October 24, 2013 Comment revision adding a cross-reference to new Rule 151 published with the Court's Order at 43 Pa.B. 6655 (November 9, 2013).

Source

The provisions of this Rule 150 adopted December 30, 2005, effective August 1, 2006, 36 Pa.B. 181; amended October 24, 2013, effective January 1, 2014, 43 Pa.B. 6654. Immediately preceding text appears at serial pages (360839) to (360841).

1-39

Rule 151. Bench Warrant Procedures When Witness is Under Age of 18 Years.

(A) In a court case when a bench warrant for a witness under the age of 18 years is executed, except as provided in this rule, the case is to proceed in accordance with the procedures in Rule 150.

(B) Upon execution of the warrant for a minor witness, the arresting officer immediately shall inform the proper judicial officer and a parent or guardian of the minor witness of the arrest of the minor witness.

(C) *Execution of Bench Warrant in County of Issuance*

(1) If the judicial officer who issued the bench warrant, or another judicial officer designated by the president judge or by the president judge's designee, is not available to conduct the bench warrant hearing without unnecessary delay, the minor witness shall be taken before the on-call judge of the court of common pleas.

(a) The on-call judge shall determine whether to release the witness or to detain the witness pending the bench warrant hearing. If the bench warrant specifically orders detention of the minor witness, the on-call judge shall not release the witness.

(b) If the on-call judge determines the witness must be detained, the witness shall be detained in a detention facility. The on-call judge shall notify the parent or guardian of the minor witness of the detention.

(2) The minor witness shall not be detained without a bench warrant hearing on that bench warrant longer than 24 hours, or the close of the next business day if the 24 hours expires on a non-business day.

(D) *Execution of Bench Warrant Outside County of Issuance*

(1) The minor witness shall be taken before a common pleas court judge of the county of arrest without unnecessary delay and in no case later than the end of the next business day.

(2) The judge shall identify the minor witness as the subject of the bench warrant, decide whether detention as a minor witness is necessary, and order that arrangements be made immediately to transport the minor witness to the county of issuance.

(3) If transportation cannot be arranged immediately, the minor witness shall be released unless the bench warrant specifically orders detention of the witness. In this case, the minor witness shall be detained in an out-of-county detention facility.

(4) If detention is ordered, the minor witness shall be brought to the county of issuance within 72 hours from the execution of the bench warrant.

(5) If the time requirements of this paragraph are not met, the minor witness shall be released.

1-40

Comment

This rule was adopted in 2013 to establish the procedures when a witness subject to a bench warrant is under the age of 18. The procedures following the execution of a bench warrant set forth in Rule 150 apply to cases when the witness is under the age of 18, except as otherwise provided in this rule.

Paragraph (B) ensures that the judicial officer who issued the bench warrant is aware that the minor witness has been arrested, and that a parent or guardian of the arrested minor witness is notified of the arrest.

The procedures in paragraph (C) for cases in which the bench warrant is executed in the county of issuance, recognize the need, when the issuing judicial officer is unavailable, to conduct the bench warrant hearing, for the common pleas court judge who is on call to determine whether a minor witness may be released or must be detained. If the minor witness is detained, the bench warrant hearing must be held no later than the end of the next business day. If the bench warrant hearing is not conducted within this time period, the minor witness must be released.

The minor witness may not be detained in an adult facility pending a bench warrant hearing.

In cases in which the bench warrant is executed outside the county of issuance, the minor witness must be transported to the county of issuance within 72 hours of the execution of the bench warrant, and the bench warrant hearing must be conducted by the end of the next business day.

As used in this rule, "minor witness" means a witness who is under the age of 18 years, and "proper judicial officer" means the judicial officer who issued the bench warrant, or, another judicial officer designated by the president judge or by the president judge's designee.

Official Note: Adopted October 24, 2013, effective January 1, 2014.

Committee Explanatory Reports:

Final Report explaining the October 24, 2013 adoption of new Rule 151 providing procedures for bench warrants when a witness is under the age of 18 published with the Court's Order at 43 Pa.B. 6655 (November 9, 2013).

Source

The provisions of this Rule 151 adopted October 24, 2013, effective January 1, 2014, 43 Pa.B. 6654.

[Next page is 2-1.]

1-42

Manufactured by Amazon.ca
Acheson, AB

13299859R00039